WRITING MATH

A Project-Based Approach

by

Sharon Z. Draznin

GoodYearBooks

An Imprint of ScottForesman
A Division of HarperCollinsPublishers

GoodYearBooks are available for most basic curriculum subjects plus many enrichment areas. For more GoodYearBooks, contact your local bookseller or educational dealer. For a complete catalog with information about other GoodYearBooks, please write:

GoodYearBooks
ScottForesman
1900 East Lake Avenue
Glenview, IL 60025

Illustrations by Yoshi Miyake.
Design by Barb Rohm Design.

ISBN 0-673-36127-6
1 2 3 4 5 6 7 8 9 -PT- 02 01 00 99 98 97 96 95

ACKNOWLEDGEMENTS

Many thanks are owed to all of the students who have sat before me and with me during all the years I've taught. They have truly been an inspiration to me and have been a catalyst for many of the activities presented in this book. As I hope they have learned from me, so I have learned much from them.

I would also like to acknowledge the expertise and professionalism of my various teammates through the years at Washington School in Evanston, Illinois. They have assisted me in bringing many of the ideas contained in this book to fruition. Also, thanks go to Sister Linda Jackim, who has been unfailing in both her support and knowledge. Last, but not least, I would like to thank my husband for his tremendous support and encouragement. He has nurtured me and allowed me the freedom which has been absolutely necessary in order to make the ideas for this book become a reality.

It is my hope for you, the reader, that your copy of this book will become dog-eared and worn from long use. Good luck!

TABLE OF CONTENTS

CHAPTER ONE **PAGE 5**

A Miniature Math Museum

The concept of mathematics and numbers being all around us, embedded throughout our everyday lives, is the theme of this chapter. Students are asked to bring to school either pictures of or actual small objects which have numbers on them. Examples are: pages from a catalogue, a phone book, license plate, receipt, etc.. A classroom "museum" is set up to display these items. The writing component of this chapter asks students to write about their contribution to the "museum" and to justify why they chose their particular item/s to display.

CHAPTER TWO **PAGE 33**

The Apple Doesn't Fall Far From the Tree

This is a chapter for fall which uses the mathematical ideas of counting, graphing, weighing, measuring, and also includes cooking. The language arts component uses writing about the tastes, textures, and uses of apples as well as incorporating sequential writing about the steps followed in preparing a recipe.

CHAPTER THREE **PAGE 51**

Writing Number Stories

This chapter teaches students how to write addition, subtraction, multiplication, division, and fraction stories. Students are asked to use a context such as: money, animals, flowers, or toys whenever they write a number story. They also generate specific numbers and write number stories using those numbers. Correct sentence structure and punctuation usage are emphasized in the writing component of this chapter. A classroom book of number stories is compiled. Use this chapter throughout the year. As each computation skill is taught, add the "Writing Number Stories" component.

CHAPTER FOUR
December Holiday Fun

PAGE 65

The overall goal for this chapter is listening and following directions. This chapter contains a paper folding activity: making a box. This box can be decorated by using sponges cut into pattern block shapes and dipped in paint. A special holiday gift can be placed in this box. Mathematically, this chapter addresses the concepts of fractions and geometric shapes. The writing component includes making a holiday card with a poem inside as the "message." Poetry writing and listening activities are extensions of this chapter. The paper folding is extended into origami and includes two holiday projects which provide additional resources for both students and teachers.

CHAPTER FIVE
Toothpicks and Marshmallows, Straws and Clay: Constructing Polygons

PAGE 97

This chapter consists of "building" two and three dimensional shapes using miniature marshmallows and toothpicks then naming the shapes. The writing component focuses on descriptive writing as students are asked to compose riddles entitled "Who Am I?" This activity can be expanded into another writing activity entitled, "Painting With Words." The math work can be expanded into creating rigid structures and estimation. Descriptive and narrative writing assignments follow.

CHAPTER SIX
Chinese New Year or Gung Hey Fat Choy!

PAGE 117

The mathematics component of this chapter involves counting forward and backward by 12 using four digit numbers (years). Students also become familiar with the various animals which make up the Chinese Zodiac. Research reports on the animals are the writing component of this chapter. Students working in pairs will address the physical characteristics of these animals, their origins, what they eat, where they live, and any other information which they consider to be significant. All animals except the dragon are real.

CHAPTER SEVEN
Trash Bashing

PAGE 145

The concepts of numeration or counting, weighing, data collection, and graphing are the focus of this chapter. Students will collect a week' s worth of classroom trash, sort it, count it, weigh it and extrapolate the amounts to include the entire school for the entire school year. Students will write descriptively about what they've done in math class in addition to learning correct letter writing format. They will write persuasive letters to adults urging them to recycle. Extensions of this activity include using the recycled material to create a "junk sculpture," decorating recycling boxes for other classrooms and writing instructions for their use, as well as a visit to a community recycling center.

CHAPTER EIGHT
Growing Plants

PAGE 165

This chapter centers on measurement and graphing. Students will grow either one classroom plant or bulb, or individual plants. They will estimate, measure and graph the growth on a regular basis. The writing component of this chapter involves keeping a scientific journal, an objective day-by-day account of what they see as their plant grows.

CHAPTER NINE
The White Elephant Sale

PAGE 181

"The White Elephant Sale" offers practical experience in using money. Students will bring several old toys or books to school for the purpose of selling them to classmates. They will gain experience with buying and selling, using money, pricing, and making change. The writing activity is a sequential writing paper entitled, "The White Elephant Sale: How We Did It!" This activity includes composing and writing ads prior to the sale urging fellow classmates to buy a particular piece of "merchandise." A classroom book incorporating the students' ads and articles can be published as well.

CHAPTER TEN
A Potpourri of Ideas: Discovery Stations

PAGE 197

This activity can be two or three days in length and requires setting up six "stations" throughout the classroom. Each station addresses a particular math concept. After their rotation through the six stations is complete, students will write a report about what they discovered. They will also write about their favorite activity and tell why they liked it.

INTEGRATING MATH AND LANGUAGE ARTS

Introduction

SO OFTEN, WHEN MEETING WITH PARENTS OF STUDENTS IN ANY CLASSROOM, I've heard the comment, "Math! No wonder my child is having difficulty. I hated math too when I was a child." The activities in this book grew out of a philosophical base whose aim it is to transform the negative feelings many adults and children have towards math into a love of math and an appreciation for its usefulness in our everyday lives.

The United States is quickly moving out of first position as a global industrial leader, in part because of the lack of a skilled and prepared workforce. All too frequently, employers have to institute remedial writing and mathematics programs for new employees. Often students take only the minimum amount of math courses required for high school graduation. We can expect to compete in world markets in today's highly technological society only if American youngsters begin to see the value of advanced mathematics courses as well as overcome their fear or dislike of math.

We, as educators, parents and administrators, can excite and interest children in math, beginning with their earliest school experiences. As children discover the usefulness and pervasiveness of math in their everyday lives, they will become able to utilize and apply it with confidence and enjoyment. This book has been written to help a child begin his or her first steps toward reaching these goals.

STATEMENT OF PURPOSE

THE PURPOSE OF THIS BOOK IS TO PROVIDE TEACHERS a means by which to link together two ordinarily quite disparate subjects: mathematics and language arts. The National Council of Teachers of Mathematics, in the Standards (1989, page 26), states:

> In grades K-4, the study of mathematics should include numerous opportunities for communication so that students can
>
> ➤ relate physical materials, pictures and diagrams to mathematical ideas;
>
> ➤ reflect on and clarify their thinking about mathematical ideas and situations

➤ relate their everyday language to mathematical language and symbols;

➤ realize that representing, discussing, reading, writing, and listening to mathematics are a vital part of learning and using mathematics.

The activities in this book are not designed to be a total curriculum. They can instead be used to supplement and complement any math curriculum. Most activities involve cooperative learning groups, either partners or small groups of three to four students. These groupings help students to build self-esteem, to complete a task and do it well, and to have successful experiences in school.

Students can be paired or grouped in many ways. You might pair a girl and a boy, a weaker and a stronger student, two students who are wearing the same color shirt or blouse, two students whose names begin with the same letter, or allow students to select their own partners. The possibilities are endless. You may also find that some students do not work well together, and you may have to assist those students so that they find suitable partners or are placed in groups that will function effectively.

This book consists of math-initiated projects which incorporate strong language arts components. The projects and activities are suitable for kindergarten, first, second, and third grade students. Parents, principals, administrators, and either math or language arts coordinators will find this book useful, helpful and exciting.

HOW TO USE THIS BOOK

The thesis that mathematics is part of our everyday lives—indeed, that it permeates our lives—will become readily apparent as one uses this book. Just think about going to the grocery store, figuring out the interest on a loan or savings account, computing mileage on your car, ordering from a catalogue, making a phone call, reading a graph in the newspaper, using a calculator, creating a budget, and so on. There are ten chapters arranged in a "school year" sequence—fall to spring. This arrangement enables the classroom teacher to use one chapter a month, September through June. Many of the projects or sets of activities last five to six school days. They employ materials commonly available in the classroom or easily brought from home. The projects contain interesting, engaging and exciting activities which promote active involvement using manipulatives. The mathematics concepts cover a wide variety of topics, ranging from number awareness to basic arithmetic operations, to fractions, geometry, using money, measurement, and graphing.

The written components of the chapters in this book incorporate a variety of skills, such as scientific journal writing and persuasive letter writing. Stress is placed upon the use of correct capitalization and punctuation, as it is developmentally appropriate.

Together, the mathematics and language arts strands of this book fulfill the communication standard of the NCTM by facilitating meaningful mathematics learning while at the same time giving students the opportunity to clarify their thinking through written work. Any primary teacher, administrator, or parent who is interested in broadening mathematics teaching and extending math concepts to include cross-curricular activities will find this book useful.

In addition to linking mathematics and language arts, the monthly projects in this book provide ample opportunity for incorporating art projects, oral expression and even science and social studies concepts. The interesting part of all of this cross-curricular teaching is that mathematics is the initiating strand of the activity rather than being merely an afterthought—again vividly illustrating the fact that math is an integral and pervasive part of our everyday lives.

The chapters in this book are arranged in an easy-to-follow, "teacher-friendly" format for the busy primary teacher. The lessons, which are best implemented in a sequential order (as presented), are designed to be completed in forty-five minute to one hour classroom sessions. Each chapter contains a week's worth or more of teacher instructions for both the math and language arts activities (art, science, and/or social studies where appropriate), student worksheets and ideas for extending the activities (again, when appropriate).

It would be useful to set up a book display using the activities bibliography found at the back of the book prior to beginning each lesson. Also, reading one of the suggested books would be an appropriate introduction or supplementary activity to "set the tone" for the chapter. Integrating books from the activities bibliography into the daily lessons would be another way to fully utilize the suggested book list.

A math-based literature bibliography can also be found in the back of this book. It will be particularly useful as it is divided into major headings, such as Problem Solving and Measurement, and then into subheadings such as estimation, number concepts and relationships, weighing, and time. Each chapter has references leading the teacher to those headings and subheadings which would be especially useful when teaching the designated concepts in that particular chapter.

Each chapter also contains instructions and illustrations for creating materials either for demonstration purposes or for specific student lessons. It would be helpful to try out the projects prior to teaching them to the students.

The author encourages students to be independent workers, students who can get what they need to begin to work. Therefore, materials are placed where students can pick them up. This procedure allows teachers to spend time teaching rather than distributing materials. It provides students with the opportunity to get up and move around for an acceptable reason. Setting up materials ahead of time enables the teacher to serve as a facilitator for learning rather than as an "imparter of knowledge." The teacher sets up the learning environment by placing materials where the students have easy access to them so that they can then "explore and discover." The teacher is able to assist students by listening to and guiding conversations and by assessing through observation. These are practices that the NCTM standards advocate and that reflect the author's general philosophy of children's learning.

SUMMARY OF CHANGES IN CONTENT AND EMPHASIS IN K-4 MATHEMATICS

- ➤ increased attention
- ➤ instructional practices
- ➤ use of manipulative materials
- ➤ cooperative work
- ➤ discussion of mathematics
- ➤ questioning
- ➤ justification of thinking
- ➤ writing about mathematics
- ➤ problem solving approach to instruction
- ➤ content integration
- ➤ use of calculators and "computers"

From *NCTM Curriculum & Evaluation Standards* (Reston, VA: 1989), page 20.

CHAPTER ONE

A Miniature Math Museum

INTRODUCTION:

The broad aim of this chapter is to enhance students' awareness of numbers. Progressing through the chapter may take a week or longer, but the individual activities take only a short part of the total math class time. (On the first day, the activity may take longer than on subsequent days.) A classroom display can be used at additional times throughout the year, particularly when studying measurement, fractions, and two- and three-dimensional shapes.

For this chapter, you may want to review books in the Mathematics-Based Literature Bibliography under the section entitled "Numbers." The references for "Numeration and Counting" and "Number Concepts and Relationships" should be especially helpful.

DAY 1

Numbers on Display

Math Objective:

Students will become aware of the prevalence and importance of numbers in daily life.

Materials and Preparation:

1. Prepare a display area. This could be a bulletin board, a large sheet of butcher paper or a very large box top.

2. Cut out letters or make a strip sign that says "Room____'s Miniature Math Museum."

3. Tell students to look around their homes for items with numbers on them that can be brought to school. Some examples include pages from a phone book or catalog, a bill for a meal at a restaurant, a grocery store receipt, an old automobile license plate, or a phone bill.

4. Prepare a 12" x 18" piece of tagboard for each student. Create an inch-wide border on each piece.

Activity:

Distribute one piece of tagboard to each student. Ask students to glue their items with numbers on them to the tagboard and decorate the border with mathematical symbols, shapes, patterns, or any other mathematical representation. Students may then bring their tagboard pieces to the display area one at a time. As they bring up their completed piece, have them tell the class about the numbers on it.

From *Writing Math: A Project-Based Approach*, published by GoodYear Books. Copyright © 1995 Sharon Z. Draznin

DAY 2

Why This Display is Important

Language Arts Objective:

Students will write about what they have brought to display for the "Miniature Math Museum." They will justify in writing what they have brought.

Materials and Preparation:

Reproduce two or three pages of writing paper from page 29 for each student.

Activity:

Distribute the paper and give directions for writing about what they have brought. If necessary, give the students a "starter," such as: "I brought_____to school because _____." (See sample page.) Ask the students to contribute words which they think they will need to write their justification stories. Put the vocabulary list on the chalkboard. (Remind students about correct capitalization and punctuation when writing.) Save these stories and compile them into a class book. (See Chapter Two for suggestions on making a book.)

After the written assignment has been completed and before compiling the sheets into a class book, have students share their information. They gather in front of the display while each student points out her/his contribution and explains why the object is appropriate for display in a miniature math museum.

Be sure to point out to students the pervasiveness of numbers in our everyday lives, from phone numbers, to grocery receipts, from classroom numbers, to recipes—ad infinitum!

TEACHER NOTE:

A display of this type can be repeated for fractions, measurement, and arrays (preparation for multiplication) as well as two- and three-dimensional shapes.

Name: _____

Date: _____

Name of my object:

_____

I brought

_____

_____

_____

to display in our Miniature Math Museum. I brought it because

_____

_____

_____

_____

_____

_____

TEACHER NOTE:

Have copies of this sheet in a box next to the museum. During the week, students bring in objects to display. They can take a sheet, fill it out, and hand it in for inclusion in the class book.

DAY 3

Visiting a Museum

Language Arts Objective:

Students will visit a community museum and complete a worksheet related to their visit.

Materials and Preparation:

The teacher will make the necessary arrangements for the field trip. These arrangements should include:

- calling the museum to set up a convenient date and time for the students' visit
- obtaining maps of the museum if they are available
- reserving and confirming transportation
- distributing a field trip permission letter to parents/guardians of all students
- providing a name tag for each student and parent chaperone
- assigning students to small groups for chaperone supervision
- arranging for a docent or curator who will explain the "inner workings" of a museum and address the following questions:

How is a museum organized?

Who makes decisions about what is to be displayed?

How are materials acquired for a display?

What is involved in preparing a display?

How is money raised to support the museum?

How are educational programs prepared?

- reproducing a sufficient number of copies of the student worksheet (pages 14-15) and chaperone sheet (page 12) as well as provide a sufficient number of pencils for student use
- sending a reminder note home the day before the field trip

TEACHER NOTE:

If this is to be a full day's trip, lunch arrangements also need to be made.

Activity:

The students, teacher, and chaperones visit a community museum. Students listen to the docent or curator, take notes on their worksheet, and tour the museum. Upon your return to school, have a discussion about the questions listed above. Record student responses on large chart paper. Pose this question to the students:

1. In what ways is our miniature math museum similar to and different from the museum we visited today?

2. Did your group discover anything about the museum that you want to share?

Field Trip Permission Slip

On_____, 199_____ our class will be taking an educational

field trip to _____museum. We will leave at _____ a.m. and

return to school by ___ p.m.. Transportation will be provided by bus. Cost of the trip is

$_____ per child. On the day of the trip, please dress your child appropriately for the

weather and send a sack lunch with a disposable drink container. If

_____ has permission to go on this trip, please sign below.

Teacher:

Parent/Guardian: _____   Date: _____

Field Trip Reminder Note

Dear Parent/Guardian:

Tomorrow is our field trip to_____museum. Please be sure your child

has returned his or her signed permission slip and paid the fee for the trip. Remember to

dress your child appropriately for the weather and to send a sack lunch including a drink

in a disposable container. Please do not send a lunch box, thermos or jar. We want to dis-

pose of our lunch containers after eating so we won't have to carry anything around in

the afternoon.

Thank you for your cooperation,

Sincerely,

From *Writing Math: A Project-Based Approach*, published by GoodYear Books. Copyright © 1995 Sharon Z. Draznin

Chaperone Sheet

Dear Mr./Mrs./Ms.

Thank you so much for joining us today on our trip to

_____.

The trip will last from _____ a.m. to _____ a.m./p.m.

You will be responsible for the following students today:

1. _____

2. _____

3. _____

4. _____

5. _____

After our whole group orientation meeting in the auditorium, you may decide together which exhibits to visit and in what order. **Please keep your group of students together and assist them in finding the answers to the questions on their worksheets.**

Please be prompt in gathering back together at _____ location by _____ o'clock for the return trip to school. Attached is a map of the museum and a listing of special displays.

I hope you and your students enjoy the day! Again, thank you!

Sincerely,

OPTIONAL:
We will meet for lunch at _____ o'clock in the museum cafeteria.

From *Writing Math: A Project-Based Approach*, published by GoodYear Books. Copyright © 1995 Sharon Z. Draznin

Name Tag

MUSEUM DETECTIVE

Name: _____

School: _____

Address: _____

Phone: _____

Museum Worksheet

Name: _____

Date: _____

1. How is the museum organized?

_____

_____

_____

_____

2. How do they get things to display?

_____

_____

_____

_____

3. How do they decide what to display? Where do they keep things they don't want to display?

_____

_____

_____

From *Writing Math: A Project-Based Approach*, published by GoodYear Books. Copyright © 1995 Sharon Z. Draznin

4. Who sets up the exhibits? What training do they have?

_____

_____

_____

_____

5. How does a museum get money?

_____

_____

_____

_____

6. How do museums help adults and children learn about what's in them?

_____

_____

_____

_____

The Museum Re-visited

Language Arts Objective:

Students will write and draw pictures about their museum visit.

Materials and Preparation:

Students need fresh copies of their museum worksheets and drawing paper.

Activity:

Have students copy their museum worksheets so that neat copies can be displayed around the miniature math museum. In addition, have them draw their favorite community museum display or object. After students complete their work, ask them to share and explain their pictures. If several students have the same favorite display or object picture, they can be grouped together for sharing.

TEACHER NOTE:

Students' drawings can be framed with construction paper. Have students use an 8 1/2" by 11" piece of paper for their drawings. When the drawings are complete, instruct students to measure and draw a 1 1/2" border around another piece of paper (illustration 1). This should be a 9" x 12" piece of colored construction paper. Once the border is drawn, fold the paper the "long way" or in a "hot dog fold" with the lined border on the outside. Students now cut along the border line that was drawn (illustration 2). When the sheet is unfolded, a frame is ready. Tape the 8 1/2" x 11" drawing inside the frame.

From *Writing Math: A Project-Based Approach*, published by GoodYear Books. Copyright © 1995 Sharon Z. Draznin

Paper Frame

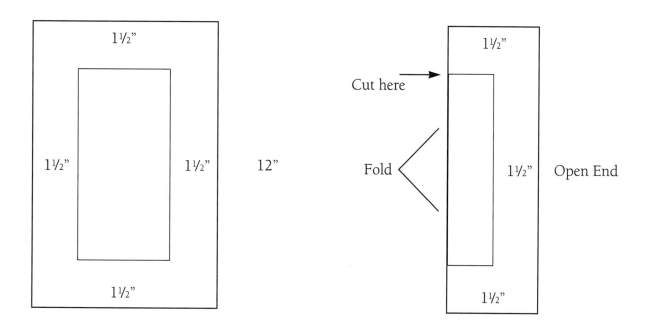

Illustration 1

Illustration 2
("Hot dog" fold)

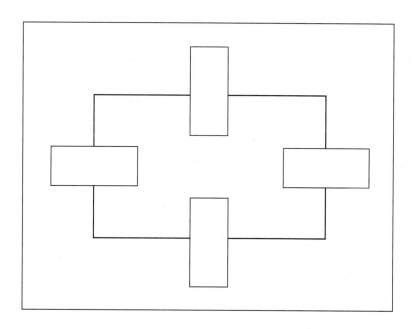

Back View

From Writing Math: A Project-Based Approach, published by GoodYear Books. Copyright © 1995 Sharon Z. Draznin

Finishing Up Our Booklets

Language Arts Objective:

Students complete a field trip booklet.

Materials and Preparation:

Copy and collate the "Field Trip Booklet" on pages 19 to 26 for each student.

Activity:

Students work on completing each page of the booklet either individually or in small groups. Directions for the cover and other pages are given on each page. The booklet may require two days to complete. Students can share their booklets with one another and the completed booklet can be sent home.

TEACHER NOTE:

While copying the following pages for the booklet, make a copy with directions for yourself. Then fold back the directions and make copies for the students. This way the directions will not appear on student copies.

Cover Illustration:

Students draw and color streets, traffic signals, students' faces in windows, driver, trees, sky, sun, etc.

Page 1

Field Trip Booklet

On_____,_____,_____

I went to _____ Museum with
my class.

Students draw the outside of the museum here.

From *Writing Math: A Project-Based Approach*, published by GoodYear Books. Copyright © 1995 Sharon Z. Draznin

Field Trip Booklet

I took _____, _____,

_____, and _____ with me.

Students draw their lunch bag, museum worksheet, pencil, and anything else they took along.

Page 3

On the trip I sat next to _____ and

_____.

Students draw themselves and their seat partner/s.

On the way there, I looked out the window. I saw_____.

Students draw any object(s) of interest they noticed on the way to the museum.

Field Trip Booklet

These were the people in my group: _____,

_____, _____,

_____ and_____.

Our chaperone was _____

Students draw their chaperone and group members. They write the appropriate name under each drawing. List the names of chaperones on the chalkboard so students can copy the one they need.

I ate my lunch at the museum. Here's what I had for lunch. I had

_____

_____

From *Writing Math: A Project-Based Approach*, published by GoodYear Books. Copyright © 1995 Sharon Z. Draznin.

Students draw their lunch on the placemat. It would be helpful to write a list of common lunch-time foods on the chalkboard, such as sandwich, chips, fruit, cookies, etc. Students can then label their foods.

Field Trip Booklet

At the museum I saw_____

_____

From *Writing Math: A Project-Based Approach*, published by GoodYear Books. Copyright © 1995 Sharon Z. Draznin

Students draw their view of a room or section of the museum with objects on display.

Page 8

26

DAY 6

Please Visit our Classroom Math Museum

Introduction:

The mathematics objective addressed in this activity is the importance and prevalence of numbers in our everyday lives.

Objective:

Students will invite other classrooms to visit the Miniature Math Museum. They will need to discuss dates, times, and length of visits in order to set up a schedule.

Materials and Preparation:

1. Make a copy of the invitation (page 28) and have a student color it.
2. Distribute it to classrooms in your building. Discuss possible dates and length of visits with the students. After the discussion, set up a schedule for visiting the "Miniature Math Museum." Discuss what a museum docent does.

3. Remind students of the role of the docent on their museum trip. Together, create a possible "script" to use as they act as docents for their own museum. Ask students, "How would you explain our miniature math museum to other students? What would you like them to know? Why did we decide to make a museum with all sorts of numbers in it?" Then have half of the class be visitors and a volunteer from the remainder of the class practice being the docent. After some time, switch roles.

TEACHER NOTE:

Some students may be uncomfortable being a docent. It is probably best to select only those students who are comfortable in the role. Also, several students may want to share the role for each visiting classroom. That way, more students are able to have a turn.

After the visitation schedule is confirmed, assign docent(s) to each visiting class. As the class enters, the docent(s) guide them to the display, explain it (using the script if desired), and answer any questions. When the question and answer period has concluded, the docent(s) will thank the class for coming to view the museum and escort the visitors to the door.

Invitation to Visit Room_____'s Miniature Math Museum

Please come to see our Miniature Math Museum. We can give you a guided tour. Sign up for a time below. Come to Room_____and see examples of the many ways numbers are a part of your everyday life!

DATE	TIME	ROOM

TEACHER NOTE:

Make a copy of this schedule and use it to assign docents to groups of visitors. Have a student color this invitation before it circulates.

From *Writing Math: A Project-Based Approach*, published by GoodYear Books. Copyright © 1995 Sharon Z. Drazmin

CHAPTER TWO

The Apple Doesn't Fall Far From the Tree

INTRODUCTION:

The mathematics skills featured in this chapter include counting and comparing numbers, measurement, and graphing. This project will take six or more days, depending on how involved you and your students become.

In order to have enough apples for all the activities, divide the apples brought in into five groups, one for each day. Buy a bag of apples to use in case of a shortfall.

DAY 1

Which is Your Favorite Apple?

Math Objective:

Students will taste various types of apples and create a graph of their favorites.

Materials and Preparation:

1. Bring a knife or apple slicer to school and have students bring several apples to school.
2. Reproduce *Note to Parents* on page 35.
3. Prepare a sheet of butcher paper or a large sheet of tagboard to be used for a demonstration graph. Use the format on page 49 as a model for the demonstration graph.
4. Reproduce an apple for each student (page 50) and a graphing sheet (page 49).

TEACHER NOTE:

Bring a variety of apples to school to "cover" for students who forget to bring their own.

Activities:

Collect the apples and count them together. Discuss their various characteristics. List vocabulary words on the chalkboard as the students suggest them. Such words as "red," "shiny," "round," "crunchy," "big," "small," and so on will undoubtedly be mentioned. Ask students if they know the names of the varieties of their apples. List these names on the board too. After washing the apples, use the apple slicer to cut them into segments. Discuss the number of segments the slicer has. Also discuss how to get enough pieces so that everyone can have a taste. Afterward, ask the students which apple was their favorite. Distribute the paper apples and have each student color an apple so it matches the real one that is his or her favorite.

While they are coloring, prepare a large classroom demonstration graph (see materials list). Ask each student to come up to the graph and paste (or use double-stick tape) their apple to the graph in the appropriate place. Each student will also make a tally mark when they place their apple on the graph. When all students have had their turn, ask them to help you convert the tally marks into numbers. Then ask: "Which variety is the favorite of this class? Which is the least favorite? Are there any ties?" Also encourage students to make comparisons by asking: "Are there more students who like yellow or red delicious apples? Are there fewer yellow delicious or green Granny Smith apples?" Ask the students to make their own comparisons and pose their questions to their classmates. Distribute the individual graph sheets and have the students make their own graphs, copying from the large classroom graph. Collect and save these sheets.

From *Writing Math: A Project-Based Approach*, published by GoodYear Books. Copyright © 1995 Sharon Z. Draznin.

Note to Parents

Date:_____

Dear Parents:

For the next few days, we will be using apples for activities involving both math and writing. Could you please send 3 or 4 apples to school with your child tomorrow? We would like a variety of apples, if possible.

Thank you for your cooperation.

Sincerely,

Room_____

How Wide Am I?

Math Objective:

Students will use a tape measure to measure the girth (or widest part) of an apple in inches and centimeters.

Materials and Preparation:

1. Bring a tape measure for each pair of students. The tape measures need to show both Standard and Metric measurements.

2. Reproduce one set of the Apples Worksheets on pages 37 and 38 for each student.

Activity:

Discuss the uses and special characteristics of a tape measure (i.e. flexibility can go around oddly-shaped objects) with the class. Point out the difference between inches and centimeters. Write the word "girth" on the chalkboard. Explain to students that measurement of the girth of an apple can be compared to measuring one's waist. Call up several pairs of students to come to the front of the classroom and measure each other's waist in both inches and centimeters. Record their measurements on the board. Have the other students find these measurements on their own tape measures.

Working in pairs, have the students measure the girth of an apple and record the measurement in both inches and centimeters on their Apple Worksheets. After everyone has measured, discuss the measurements. Ask: "Who had the widest apple? Who had the thinnest? Were there any ties?" Also ask the students to make conjectures about the relationship between girth and weight. Do they think the widest apple will also be the heaviest? Collect and save these worksheets. They will be used in other lessons. Save the apples also as they too will be used in other lessons.

TEACHER NOTE:

Partnerships can be formed in many ways. You can pair a boy with a girl or have the students count off and pair 1 and 3, 2 and 4, 5 and 7, 6 and 8, and so on. You can also allow students to choose their own partner, with the stipulation that they choose someone with whom they can work well. Establish the following "partner rules":

1. Help each other out without telling the answers.

2. If a partner makes a mistake or gets the wrong answer, ask him or her to try again.

3. Tell your partner what a good job he or she is doing.

From *Writing Math: A Project-Based Approach*, published by GoodYear Books. Copyright © 1995 Sharon Z. Draznin.

From *Writing Math: A Project-Based Approach*, published by GoodYear Books. Copyright © 1995 Sharon Z. Draznin

Name _____

The girth of my apple is

in. _____

gm. _____

How much does a whole apple weigh?

oz. _____

gm. _____

How much does a peeled apple weigh?

oz. _____

gm. _____

How much does a slice weigh?

oz. _____

gm. _____

Name _____

How much does the core weigh?

oz. _____

gm. _____

What other parts of the apple can you weigh?

The peel weighs

oz. _____

gm. _____

From *Writing Math: A Project-Based Approach*, published by GoodYear Books. Copyright © 1995 Sharon Z. Draznin

DAY 3

How Heavy Am I?

Math Objective:

Students will weigh their apples in ounces and grams using various types of scales.

Materials and Preparation:

1. You will need the Apple Worksheets from the previous lesson, a pan balance and two sets of metric weights, another scale that weighs in ounces, and a collection of several objects to be weighed.

2. Reproduce for each student "A Book About Apples and Apple Trees by _____" on pages 41 through 44.

Activity:

Show students the scales and point out the differences between them. Discuss the attribute of *weight*. Just what does it mean to *weigh* something? Call on several students to weigh an object from your small collection in both ounces and grams. Write this information on the chalkboard, explaining that *oz.* is the abbreviation for ounces and *gm.* is the abbreviation for grams.

Hand out the Apple Worksheets from the previous lesson and the booklet entitled, "A Book About Apples and Apple Trees by _____ ." Call on several pairs of students at a time to weigh and record their apples' weight. Assist if necessary. While you work with these students, have the others illustrate, staple, and read their booklet. By following this procedure, all the students will be productively occupied, freeing you to work with those students needing help with weighing.

When all the students have weighed and recorded their apples' weight, discuss the question of the relationship between girth and weight . Ask: "Is it possible to make any generalizations or draw any conclusions about the weight of an apple based on its girth?" Collect both the booklets and worksheets.

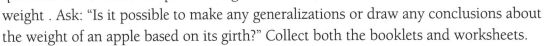

TEACHER NOTE:

Place student papers into a folder, a 12" by 18" sheet of construction paper folded in half. Have students decorate and title this folder appropriately. At the end of this project, students can take the folder and its contents home.

From *Writing Math: A Project-Based Approach*, published by GoodYear Books. Copyright © 1995 Sharon Z. Draznin

A Book About Apples and Apple Trees

By _____

From *Writing Math: A Project-Based Approach*, published by GoodYear Books. Copyright © 1995 Sharon Z. Draznin.

When a seed is in the ground, tender roots and tiny pale leaves grow from the seed. Later, a stem, more leaves, and roots branch out. Now you have a sapling, a young apple tree.

Page 1

Some apples are big. Others are small. The rest are medium-sized.

From *Writing Math: A Project-Based Approach*, published by GoodYear Books. Copyright © 1995 Sharon Z. Draznin

Apples are red, green, and yellow. Some apples have more than one color. Apples can have spots on them.

Page 3

From *Writing Math: A Project-Based Approach*, published by GoodYear Books. Copyright © 1995 Sharon Z. Draznin

You can make applesauce, apple cider, and apple juice from apples. You can make many other things from apples, too.

Page 4

44

DAY 4

Getting To The Core of Things

Math Objective:

Students will weigh other parts of their apples in both ounces and grams.

Language Arts Objective:

Students will write about the characteristics of apples, their taste, their texture, and their various uses.

Materials and Preparation:

1. You will need apples and scales, as in the lesson for day three. You will also need peelers.

2. Reproduce the writing paper on page 29 for each student. Draw a large apple on a piece of butcher paper.

Activity:

Pass out the Apple Worksheets which have been saved in the students' folders. Reproduce two sheets of writing paper on page 29 for each student. Have part of the class continue

TEACHER NOTE:

At this point, students may need extra apples so be sure to have some available. You may want to enlist the assistance of a parent volunteer for this lesson to supervise the peeling and cutting of apples.

While the scales are in use and you are rotating pairs of students to the "weighing table," have the remainder of the class work on Apples Stories. Do some vocabulary-building with students first. Ask them to describe the taste, texture, color, uses of, shape, size, etc. of apples. List the words they suggest on the large butcher paper apple (see materials list above). This butcher paper apple can be used as a chart. Have the students write descriptive stories about apples, incorporating words from the apple wall chart. Remind them to use correct punctuation. Collect and save these stories. Compile them into a classroom book so the students can share their stories with each other.

To make a classroom book, cut two 9" by 12" pieces of tagboard, one for the front cover and

one for the back cover. See the illustration for a title suggestion or use your own idea. Spiral-bind the book covers and story pages together, laminating covers first for durability. If a binding machine is unavailable, punch three holes in the covers and story pages and tie the book together with pieces of yarn.

DAY 5

We Make Amazing Applesauce!

General Objective:

Students will make applesauce.

Math Objective:

They will discuss the original recipe and figure out how to double and triple the recipe. Students will count to 12 as they rotate the handle of the food mill.

Materials and Preparation:

1. You will need the apples, sugar, cinnamon, a large pot and a large mixing spoon, a measuring cup, a food mill, if available, small paper cups or bowls, plastic spoons, a hot plate and apple slicers (either eight-segment or twelve-segment or both).

2. Write the recipe on a large sheet of chart paper and display it in the area where the cooking will take place. See page 47 for the recipe.

TEACHER NOTE:

Ask a parent volunteer or two to assist with this project.

Activity:

Review the list of products made from apples (the "Language Arts Objective" from day four the various uses of apples represent a list of products made from apples.) If students think of other products, add them to the list now. Discuss the recipe, asking students to help determine how to double or triple the recipe. Give them a choice of which slicer to use. Let them take turns measuring ingredients and stirring as the sauce cooks. (Be sure to have adult supervision near the hot plate.) After the sauce is cooked and has cooled, put it through the food mill to remove skin and seeds. Students can count twelve turns each as they rotate the handle of the mill. Serve the sauce with cinnamon, if desired.

46

From *Writing Math: A Project-Based Approach*, published by GoodYear Books. Copyright © 1995 Sharon Z. Draznin

From *Writing Math: A Project-Based Approach*, published by GoodYear Books. Copyright © 1995 Sharon Z. Draznin

APPLESAUCE

You will need:

* 8 apples
* 1/2 cup water
* 1/2 cup sugar
* cinnamon (optional)

Directions:

Using an apple slicer, cut apples into eighths or twelfths. Do not peel. Add water and simmer until soft. Stir in sugar while sauce is still hot. Put through a food mill to strain. Sprinkle with cinnamon, if you desire.

Amazing Applesauce, Step By Step

Language Arts Objective:

Students will write a sequential story about making applesauce.

Materials and Preparation:

Reproduce the Applesauce Recipe (page 47) and writing paper (page 29) for each student.

Activity:

Using the large chart paper recipe for Amazing Applesauce, review the steps in the process for making applesauce. Ask the students if they can suggest any vocabulary needed in order to write a story about their experiences. Explain that the term "sequential" means step by step, in order. Direct the students to write a sequential story entitled "We Make Applesauce" as you distribute the paper and recipe sheets. Also, have the students color and decorate the recipe sheet. Remind students to use correct punctuation as they write. Circulate and assist wherever necessary. When the class period is nearly over, collect these papers and place them in the students' "Apple Folders."

Art Extension:

Each student can create a "torn paper" apple tree using various colors of construction paper. The student should decide how many apples to place on the tree and then write that numeral on their picture. These pictures can be used as a bulletin board display.

Field Trip Extension:

The class can take a field trip to a nearby apple orchard, if possible given your geographic area. After the trip, they can write a class booklet entitled, "Our Trip to the Orchard" containing illustrated stories, or they can write a whole class experience story.

From *Writing Math: A Project-Based Approach*, published by GoodYear Books. Copyright © 1995 Sharon Z. Draznin

My Favorite Apples

Name: _____

	Red Delicious	Golden Delicious	Macintosh	Granny Smith	Winesap			
1								
2								
3								
4								
5								
6								
7								
8								
9								
10								
11								
12								

From *Writing Math: A Project-Based Approach*, published by GoodYear Books. Copyright © 1995 Sharon Z. Draznin.

CHAPTER THREE
Writing Number Stories

INTRODUCTION:

This chapter focuses simultaneously on mathematics and writing. Like Chapter One, "Creating a Miniature Math Museum," it can be revisited several times during the school year. For example, when teaching addition, have students write addition stories; when teaching subtraction, have students write subtraction stories; and so on for multiplication, division, fractions and geometry.

DAY 1

Addition in Story Form

Math/Language Arts Objective:
Students will write number stories using addition and place these stories in a context.

Materials and Preparation:
Reproduce several sheets of "My Addition Story" for each student (page 53).

Activity:

Invite students to volunteer to tell addition stories. You may need to explain to them what this means, and give an example, such as:

"One day, three alligator friends went to the movies. When they got there, they sat with four more alligator friends. How many alligator friends were in their group at the movies?"

Encourage other students to try to solve the problem posed by each student's story. Assist, if necessary, by asking questions such as: "What made you think of that answer? Can you explain your thinking? Can you think of another way to solve the problem?" Elicit a variety of addition strategies such as counting on, doubles plus one, or add tens first. An example of doubles plus one strategy is: What is 6 + 7? 6 + 6 = 12, and 7 is one more than 6, so the sum of 6 + 7 will be one more than 12, 13. Remind students that their stories must l) ask a question, and 2) make the question one that can be answered by adding. Encourage students to use correct punctuation and capitalization when writing addition stories. Also encourage them to write more than one number story.

Extensions:

Share the stories by asking for volunteers to read them aloud at the end of the writing period. Collect and save these stories. They can be bound into a class book. See Chapter Three, Day 4, for ideas on book binding.

TEACHER NOTE:

To vary the activity, have the students use their favorite number as the answer to their problem or as part of their problem. For example, if a student's favorite number is ten, then ten has to be the answer to the problem the student creates or the number ten has to be a part of the problem (one of the addends).

From *Writing Math: A Project-Based Approach*, published by GoodYear Books. Copyright © 1995 Sharon Z. Drazmin

My Addition Story

Picture This

Language Arts Objective:

Students will edit their addition stories and illustrate them on drawing paper.

Reproduce a sufficient amount of "My Addition Story" writing paper and "A Picture of My Addition Story" sheets to be used for illustrating the students' written work.

Activity:

Have some students begin to illustrate their problems. Remind them to draw clearly and to be sure to illustrate their problem exactly, showing groups joining together (the basic concept of addition). Call on other students to come up to you so that you can help them edit their problems.

TEACHER NOTE:

If you've previously read the problems, you can call up several students who have the same corrections to work on, such as capitalization or correct spelling. You'll save time and encourage students to help each other. At the same time, the other students will be occupied with illustrating their stories and will not be wasting time by waiting in line. Rotate groups of students you are helping so that at any one time one-fourth of the students are working with you and three fourths of the group are illustrating their stories.

Save these stories and illustrations to put into a classroom book. (See Day 1) Students will enjoy reading it during their free time. If there is extra time, or if some students complete their editing, recopying, and illustrating quickly, you can encourage them to write additional stories.

From *Writing Math: A Project-Based Approach*, published by GoodYear Books. Copyright © 1995 Sharon Z. Draznin

A Picture of My Addition Story

Name: _____

Date: _____

From *Writing Math: A Project-Based Approach*, published by GoodYear Books. Copyright © 1995 Sharon Z. Draznin

Can You Solve My Problem?

Math/Language Arts Objective:

Students will work in small groups, exchanging stories and solving them.

Materials and Preparation:

1. Make copies of students' number stories. Use the originals and illustrations for the classroom book.
2. Distribute copies to the "authors" of the problems. For this activity, it would be helpful if students have written more than one number story.

Activity:

Divide the class into small groups of three or four students each. Make sure to select students for each group who can work well together and learn from one another. Consider ability levels when grouping and choose a strong student for each group—one who can assume a leadership role and keep the activity moving.

Each student will take a turn presenting his or her problem. Another student in the group will try to solve the problem. Each group member should have a turn being "presenter" and "solver." If time permits, change the groupings so that students will have the opportunity to share their stories with another set of classmates.

Your role as teacher will be to circulate among the groups as a facilitator. You will want to assist students in staying focused, taking turns, keeping their voices at a conversational level, and solving any problems which may arise.

Allow some time at the end of the class session for whole group discussion. Ask the students to share what they discovered or learned from sharing and solving each other's addition number stories.

From *Writing Math: A Project-Based Approach*, published by GoodYear Books. Copyright © 1995 Sharon Z. Draznin

From *Writing Math: A Project-Based Approach*, published by GoodYear Books. Copyright © 1995 Sharon Z. Draznin

DAY 4

Number Cards and Number Stories

Math Objective:

Students continue to create and solve addition stories by playing a game using number cards.

Materials and Preparation:

1. Provide a copy of page 58 (1-10 number cards) for each student.
2. Have the students cut out these cards and write their name or initials on the back of each card. These cards can be laminated for greater durability.
3. Give each student a regular letter-sized envelope to decorate. Place the cut-out set of numbers in the envelope to be kept in the student's desk for safekeeping.

Activity:

Divide the class into pairs of students, or let students choose their partners. Each pair will combine their sets of number cards and mix them up, face down, on the playing surface. One student turns up 2 cards. The other student has to tell an addition story using the numbers on the turned up cards. Partners take turns turning up the number cards and telling a corresponding number story, and giving the answer to the number story problem.

TEACHER NOTE:

This is a game which serves several important purposes. It provides oral practice in creating number stories, it provides practice in solving basic addition problems in a fun way, and it gives students the opportunity to use partner skills; for example, learning to take turns, to help each other without telling the answer, and to praise one another for a job well done.

1-10 Number Cards

1	**2**
3	**4**
5	**6**
7	**8**
9	**10**

From *Writing Math: A Project-Based Approach*, published by GoodYear Books. Copyright © 1995 Sharon Z. Draznin

A Problem In A Box

Objective:

Students will create a shoe box display illustrating their addition problem.

Materials and Preparation:

1. Students need to bring one or more shoe boxes from home (see page 61 for the request note to parents). Send the request note home a few days before you do this project.

2. Provide colored construction paper, rulers, scissors, clay, tagboard pieces, and whatever other materials you think your students might need in order to complete this project. Some students may not bring a shoe box, so if others bring extras, each student will have one.

3. Prepare an example of a partially completed shoe box problem, which will be used for demonstration.

Activity:

Present the partially completed example of a shoe box problem which you have prepared. Show students how to cut pieces of construction paper to fit the back, sides, top and bottom, forming the background by measuring the sides of the box that will need to be covered and then cutting out paper using those measurements. Put a sample problem on the chalkboard. An example might be: "three birds were in one tree and four birds were in another tree. How many birds were in both trees?"

It might be good to pair students for this activity even though each student will be working on an individual shoe box. Pairing of students will enable them to help each other verbally by exchanging ideas and sharing their materials.

Find a space or make space to set up an assortment of materials, cafeteria style, using a long counter or table. Set out cut pieces of construction paper, tagboard, lumps of clay, and other materials listed above. Have enough small boxes or trays available for one half of your class (pairs will collect and share materials). Then have pairs of students line up together, pick up a tray or box, and collect what they need. Students should feel free to return and get more materials as necessary.

Circulate and assist students. Ask them to verbalize their problems so you can be sure they are illustrating them properly. Replenish art materials as they are used up.

When completed, these shoe box problems would make a wonderful display in your classroom, in the library, or perhaps in the school hallway on several tables with provisions made for graduated height.

Request to Parents

Dear Parents,

We are doing a special math project in school. If you have a shoe box (or two) that you are not using, please send it to school tomorrow with your child.

Thank you.

Sincerely,

Or

Dear _____,

I need to bring a shoe box to school. Do we have an old one that I can have?

Thanks !

Love,

Words To Go With A Problem In A Box

INTRODUCTION:

Introduce this activity by explaining to students that after they finish their shoe box problems they will be writing their addition problems on "cards" and placing them in front of their display. First, talk about patterns with students explaining that the border of each card will be decorated with a pattern. Elicit several responses and invite students to come to the board to draw their ideas for patterns. Ask students for suggestions for words they will be needing as they write.

Create a vocabulary list for students to refer to as they write out their problems. Finally, show a problem written numerically on the chalkboard to illustrate the transition from written words to numerical equivalencies.

Language Arts Objective:

Students will use a 4" x 6" card on which to write their shoe box problem. The card will be placed in front of each display.

Materials and Teacher Preparation:

1. Copy the sample 4" x 6" card on page 64 for each student, plus some extras to allow for student errors.

2. Prepare enough blank 4" x 6" tagboard cards for the class, plus some extras in case students make mistakes. The paper card is for practice. Once students figure out how to write their problem out correctly, it can be copied onto the tagboard card for display.

Activity:

Make sure all students have completed their shoe boxes. Continue to have materials available and circulate in order to assist the students wherever necessary. Have the 4" x 6" paper cards ready so that as students complete their shoe boxes they can pick up a sheet to write their problems on. Continue to circulate among the students, reminding them to look at the chalkboard for words they need and assisting them with unlisted words.

TEACHER NOTE:

It might be helpful to carry a small pad of paper and a pencil so that as a student requests a word, you can write it down, tear off the note paper and leave it with the student.

After students have completed their sheets and you have checked them, have tagboard cards available so that students can pick one up and copy their problem.

Number Story

From *Writing Math: A Project-Based Approach*, published by GoodYear Books. Copyright © 1995 Sharon Z. Draznin

Name: _____

Problem: _____

_____

_____

Question: _____

_____

_____

Numbers: _____ + _____ = _____

Name: Susan Smith

Problem: Two birds were sitting in a tree. Three birds were sitting in another tree.

Question: How many birds were in both trees?

Number Model: 2 + 3 = 5

TEACHER NOTE:

Make sufficient paper copies and tagboard copies so that each student can have one. Also make a few extra copies of each type.

From *Writing Math: A Project-Based Approach*, published by GoodYear Books. Copyright © 1995 Sharon Z. Draznin

CHAPTER FOUR

December Holiday Fun

INTRODUCTION:

The mathematics concepts featured in this chapter are fractions and geometric shapes. The language arts skills are listening and following directions, as well as, creative writing. It would be useful to check sections in the major bibliography for books which address patterning, fractions and geometry to use with your students.

DAY 1

Making Paper Boxes

Math Objective:

Students will construct a box simply by folding paper. In the process they will discuss fractions and geometric shapes.

Materials and Preparation:

Provide paper for folding which is approximately 8 1/2" by 11" inches. You might add some variety by making several types of paper available. For instance, plain white xerox paper could be used for practice and colored construction paper, pre-cut wrapping paper or wallpaper from discontinued pattern books could be used for the finished product.

Activity:

Give each student an 8 1/2" x 11" sheet of white paper. Explain that they will have to watch and listen very carefully in order to make their boxes. Instruct students to follow the steps with you. As you demonstrate, quickly check around the room, making sure each student is doing exactly what you are doing. Assist when necessary and/or have the students help each other.

1. Fold the paper in half (a "hamburger " fold). Make sure that all the corners are touching. Ask: "What is each part called?" (one half - 1/2) "What is the shape called?" (a rectangle) [For help, see illustrations on the next page.]

2. Fold the paper in half once again. Ask: "Now, what is each part called?" (one fourth - 1/4) "What is the shape called?" (a rectangle)

3. Now fold the rectangle that was folded in 1/4's in half. Ask: "How many parts are there now?" (8) "What is each part called?" (one eighth - 1/8) "What is the shape called?" (a rectangle)

4. Now fold the rectangle in half once more. Ask: "Can you predict how many parts there will be?" (16) "What is each part called?" (one sixteenth - 1/16) "Is the final shape still a rectangle?" (yes) Students can measure if they're not sure. This would be a good time to discuss the definition of a rectangle.

5. Open the sheet completely and put it on the table. There should be four sections across the 8 1/2" edge and four sections across the 11" edge. Fold the top four sections of the 8 1/2" side down into the middle crease. The fold the bottom four sections of the 8 1/2" section up into the middle crease. If you turn your paper sideways, you will see that you have formed two "doors," like cabinet doors, that open out from the middle of the paper.

6. Fold the outside corners into right angles. Align them with the crease that they are folding to, NOT to the edge of the paper (edge of the "door"). There will be a little more than a 1/2" gap where the triangle does not reach the edge of the paper.

7. Then fold back the long edges at the place where the "doors" meet to form a "cuff" over the corners. It helps to keep a finger on the middle of the cuff to keep it from tearing as you bend the edges back to fold.

8. Pull apart gently from the center of the "cuffs" to open the paper into a box. Shape it gently by pinching the corners and creasing the bottom folds into place. You can use a small piece of tape to secure the places on the sides where the "cuffs" do not meet. If a second, slightly smaller or slightly larger piece of paper is used, the original box can have a cover.

TEACHER NOTE:

It is suggested that this project be made at holiday time (December). This box can then be used to hold a small family gift.

From *Writing Math: A Project-Based Approach*, published by GoodYear Books. Copyright © 1995 Sharon Z. Draznin

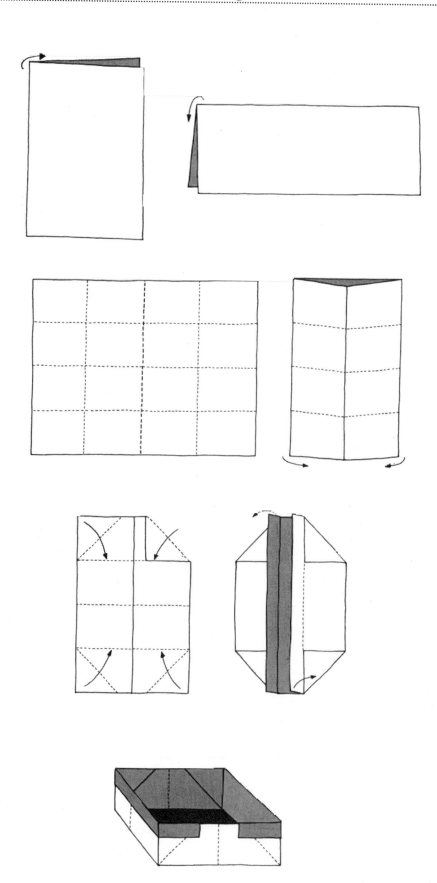

Alternate Folded Paper Box

Objective:

Students will create a folded paper box.

Math Objective:

Students will use vocabulary such as:

opposite
center point
square
triangular

Materials and Preparation:

1. Cut square sheets of paper. 8 1/2" by 8 1/2" is a good size to begin this project.

2. Have rulers or straight edges and scissors available for student use.

Activity:

Distribute one square to each student. Have students lightly draw a line from one corner of the square to the opposite (illustration 1). Do this again on the opposite corners. Explain that the point where the two lines cross is the center of the square. Have them mark this point with a pencil.

1. Fold each corner in so that it touches the center mark. (illustration 2) You now have four triangles inside a square perimeter. (Demonstrate each step as you instruct the students. Circulate and assist students as needed.)

2. Without unfolding the paper, fold each corner that touches the center point and fold it back to the middle point of its respective side. Then fold each side of the square inwards so that the middle point of the side touches the middle point of the paper. Each side can be folded in and then unfolded; the idea is to create a smaller, creased square in the larger square of the paper.

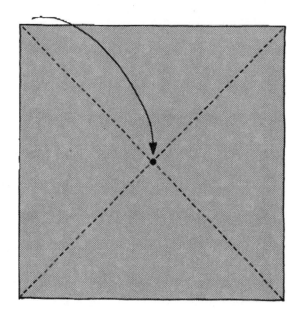

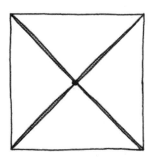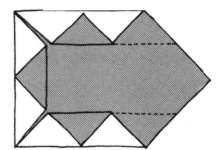

3. Unfold one side. Cut into the paper along the two fold lines that extend out from the inner creased square to the edge of the inside square. (illustration 4) Unfold the opposite side and do the same thing. (Note: only do two sides.)

4. Leave these edges flat and fold up the other two sections to form two opposite sides of the box. Next, fold the two cut sections up over the two already standing sides. This will form the other two opposite sides of the box.

5. Press the triangular sections now inside the box to the bottom, perhaps securing the last one with a drop of glue. The box is completed! As students fold their boxes, discuss the shapes which appear, for example: rectangles and triangles.

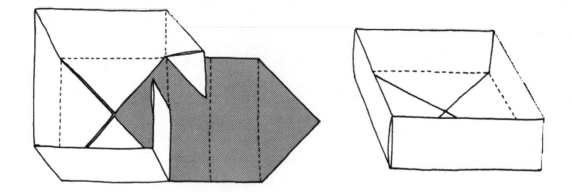

TEACHER NOTE:

These boxes are very flexible. If students wish to make a second box using 8 1/2" by 8 1/2" paper, one box will fit over the other to form a box with a lid, even though the boxes are the same size. Later, if desired, provide square sheets in other sizes so that students can experiment making differently-sized boxes and/or lids.

DAY 2

Shapes And Patterns

Math Objective:

Students will discuss patterns and geometric shapes as they decorate their paper boxes with patterns using sponges cut into shapes and dipped in paint.

Materials and Preparation:

1. Purchase a package or 2 of cellulose sponges. Cut them into the following pattern block shapes: square, triangle, trapezoid, rhombus (diamond), and hexagon. You can also add a circle and a rectangle, if desired. Cut 2 or 3 copies of each shape so that more than one student can use the same shape at the same time.

2. You will also need 3 or 4 small paint containers (blue, green, yellow and red are good color choices) that are wide enough so that students can have easy access when dipping the sponge in the paint.

3. Cover a table or counter with old newspapers and have a pail of clear water and a large sponge readily available for clean-ups. You will also need to provide another flat surface covered with newspapers where the boxes and/or boxtops can be left to dry.

4. Lastly, have a container of pattern blocks available for tracing.

Activity:

Hold up each shape and call on students to name and describe each one. Tell the students that now they will be playing a guessing game but that you are not going to tell them the rules. They must determine them by themselves. Call up several students in the following order: boy, girl, boy, girl, etc. Ask the students what they can tell you about the "line-up." After they have guessed correctly, try another example such as one involving a color pattern. For example, call up two students with red shirts, one with a blue shirt, etc. When the students have correctly guessed that pattern, invite one of them to be the "teacher" and to choose a group of students who will form a pattern. The "teacher" can then call on his/her remaining classmates to guess the pattern. Continue this activity until you are sure the students grasp the concept of a pattern. Ask for a definition of a pattern and write it on the chalkboard. Make sure the students incorporate the notion of repetition in their definition.

Explain that now they will make their own patterns as practice before sponge painting their boxes. Distribute drawing paper and ask students to take out their crayons. Place the pattern block container(s) in places where students can have easy access to them. Ask students to fold their paper in half along the longer side (this as a "hot-dog" fold). Instruct the students to create four patterns, two on each side, using the shapes previously described. They may draw them freehand or trace pattern block shapes.

Students can then color their patterns, using the paints you have prepared. Tell students that they will need to choose their favorite pattern to replicate on their box, using the sponges and paint. Give students a few minutes to get started. While most students are creating patterns on paper, call a group of four or five students to the sponge-painting area. At first, choose students who have quickly begun their patterns or those who you can tell have good ideas. Have each student bring the box or boxtop he or she made in the previous lesson. Supervise the sponge painting, making sure a pattern is followed. Direct each student to place his or her finished box(es) in the "drying area." Call on another group to sponge paint. When students return to their seats, they can complete the patterns that they were drawing on paper. These can be used later as a bulletin board display.

From *Writing Math: A Project-Based Approach*, published by GoodYear Books. Copyright © 1995 Sharon Z. Draznin

From *Writing Math: A Project-Based Approach*, published by GoodYear Books. Copyright © 1995 Sharon Z. Draznin

DAY 3

Greetings

Language Arts Objective:

Students will create a card with a poem in it to accompany their decorated box.

Materials and Preparation:

1. Duplicate at lease one sheet of writing paper (page 29) for each student as well as copies of the Santa pop-up card and the small writing paper which fits inside the card (pages 74, 75).

2. Compile a selection of books containing poems from the Activities Bibliography (page 215). Be sure to add your own favorites.

3. Bring in some greeting cards that contain poems and encourage students to do the same. Send a note home a few days prior to this lesson requesting that each child bring either a birthday or get well card to class. (See page 76)

Activity:

Discuss the concepts of poetry and rhyme with the students. Give examples of different types of poetry, read some poems to the students, and have them share poems that they know. As part of the discussion, name particular situations when one might choose to give the gift of poetic verses, especially those printed on greeting cards. Share greeting card messages, pointing out the use of poetry and the fact that poems don't always rhyme. Place the cards in a display area so that students can continue to look at them and read them.

Distribute writing paper. Explain to students that they will be making a holiday card with a message inside. The card will accompany their special box (and its contents, if any). Use the regular writing paper on page 29 for practice. Circulate among the students to assist them as needed. Encourage students to keep their poetic message brief but appropriate.

After they have written their poem, have the students get a Santa card and a piece of writing paper for inside the card. Instruct them to cut out their card and help them to fold it so it pops up. Lastly, have them copy their poem and glue the sheet inside the card.

Santa pop-up card, front side

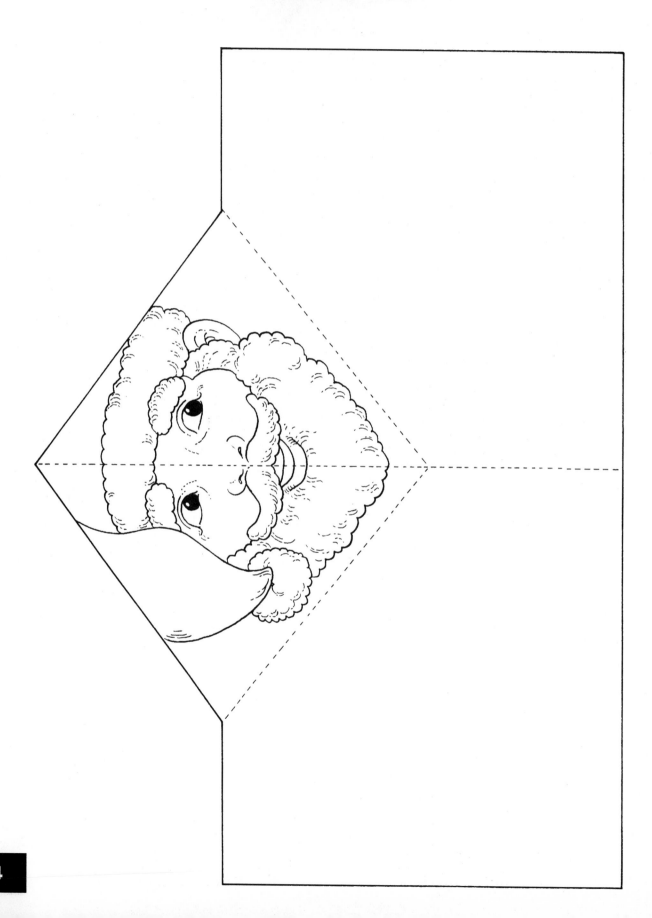

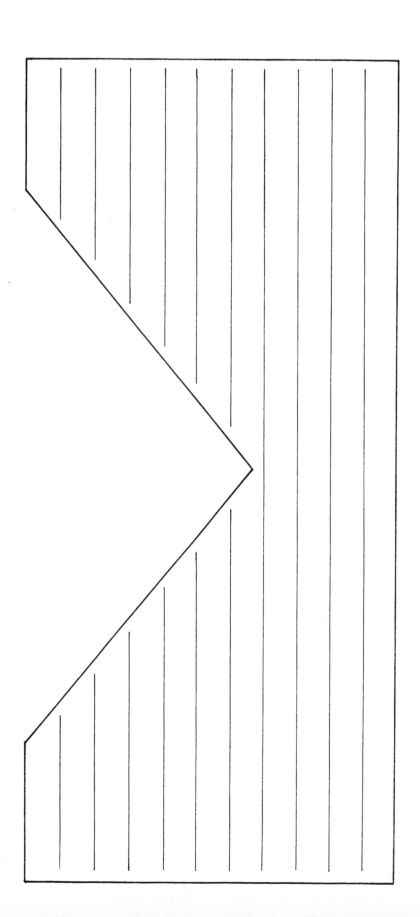

Request for Greeting Cards

Dear Parent:

We are studying poetry in our class. Since poems often appear in greeting cards, they are useful examples for our study. If you have any greeting cards, such as birthday or get-well cards, please send one or two to school with your child. The cards will be returned in about a week.

Thanks for your cooperation.

Sincerely,

From *Writing Math: A Project-Based Approach*, published by GoodYear Books. Copyright © 1995 Sharon Z. Draznin

DAY 4

Santa Claus Is Coming To Town

Language Arts Objective:

Students will create a Santa out of folded paper and then write a story about their Santa.

Materials and Preparation:

You will need the following materials for this activity:

- at least 3 sheets of 9" x 12" red construction paper per student
- 1 sheet of 9" x 12" black construction paper per student
- 1/2 sheet of 9" x 12" white construction paper per student
- 1 6" diameter paper plate per student
- aluminum foil squares - 3" x 3"
- cotton balls
- writing paper (found on page 29)

1. Cut some of the red construction paper into 12" x 2 1/2" strips. These will be used for Santa's legs. Each student will need 2 strips.

2. Cut additional red construction paper into 12" x 1/2" strips. These strips will be used for Santa's arms. Each student will need 2 of these strips.

3. Cut a 9" x 2 1/4" strip from the black construction paper to be used for Santa's belt. Use the patterns on pages 79-81 for Santa's mittens, boots, hat, and belt buckle.

4. Use the half sheet of white construction paper for the mittens, one sheet of red construction paper for the hat, one sheet of black construction paper for the boots, and the 3" x 3" aluminum foil square for the belt buckle.

TEACHER NOTE:

This activity and the accompanying writing activity may extend over two days, depending on the attention span of the children and the time that is available.

Activity:

First, distribute one 9" x 12" sheet of red construction paper to each student. Ask the students to identify the shape of the paper. Distribute the arms, legs, belt, and head. Have students identify these shapes as well. Instruct students to fold this sheet into a "fan" using back and forth folds approximately 1 1/2" wide (8 sections). This sheet will be Santa's body.

Second, distribute two 12" x 1 1/2" strips (the arms) to each student. While holding the two strips together, students should fold them in the same way as they folded the body. Using glue, paste, or staples, instruct the students to attach the arms to the body at the "shoulders".

Third, distribute two 12" x 2 1/2" strips (the legs) to each student. Repeat the fan-folding procedure and attach these strips to the bottom of Santa's body to form the legs.

Fourth, distribute one small paper plate to each student. Instruct them to attach it to the top of Santa's body to form his head. It is probably best to use a stapler for this step.

Finally, distribute the black strip (9" x 2 1/4") and demonstrate how to glue it to the middle of Santa's body to form his belt. Use the patterns on pages 79-81, and the remaining construction paper and aluminum foil to complete Santa's mittens, boots, hat, and belt buckle. Attach these parts in the appropriate places on Santa's body.

Santa should look like this: ➤

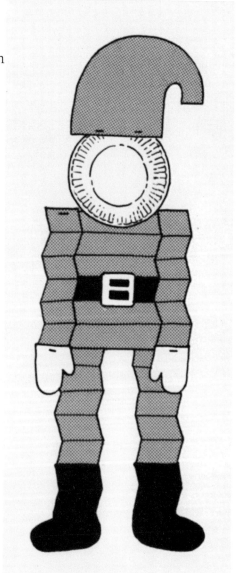

Now it's time for the trim. Instruct students to glue a cotton ball on the end of Santa's hat. They can also trim the tops of Santa's boots and mittens with cotton balls. Show students how to gently pull the cotton balls apart. This will help to make them go further. Buttons can be drawn on Santa's jacket, and additional cotton balls can be used to form a beard and moustache. Students can use crayons or markers to draw in Santa's face. Some students may want to make Santa carrying a sack of toys. Provide extra paper for this option. Encourage students to use their imaginations.

As soon as they complete their Santa, they can pick up a sheet of writing paper. Direct students to write about their Santa. They might describe his appearance, or write about the gifts that he is bringing, or about his life in the North Pole. This is an exciting project so students' imaginations should really be working. Circulate among the students during this writing period and assist wherever necessary. At the end of this activity, display the students' Santas together with their stories. "Santa Claus Is Coming To Town" makes an appropriate title for this bulletin board.

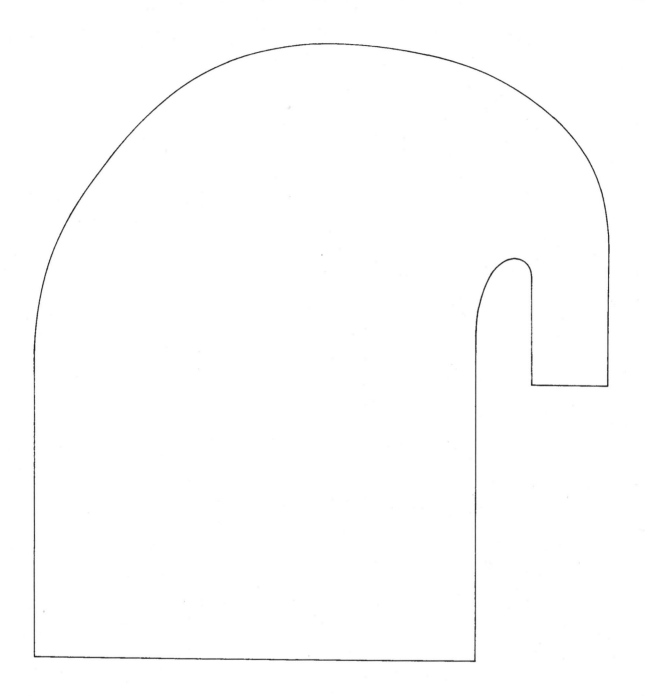

Santa Hat

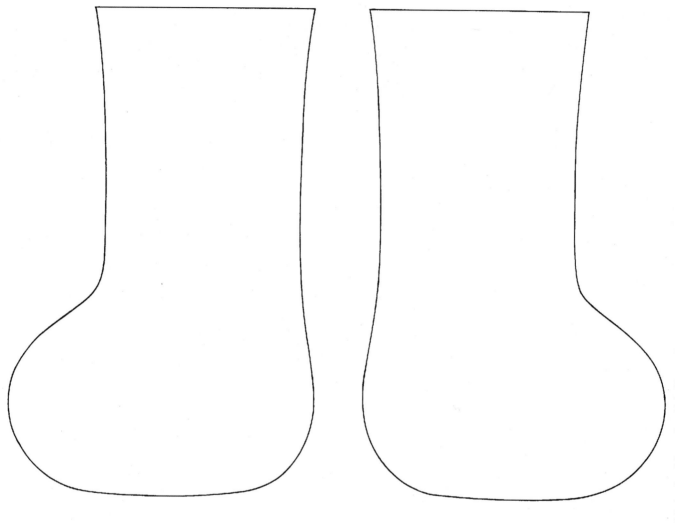

Santa Boots

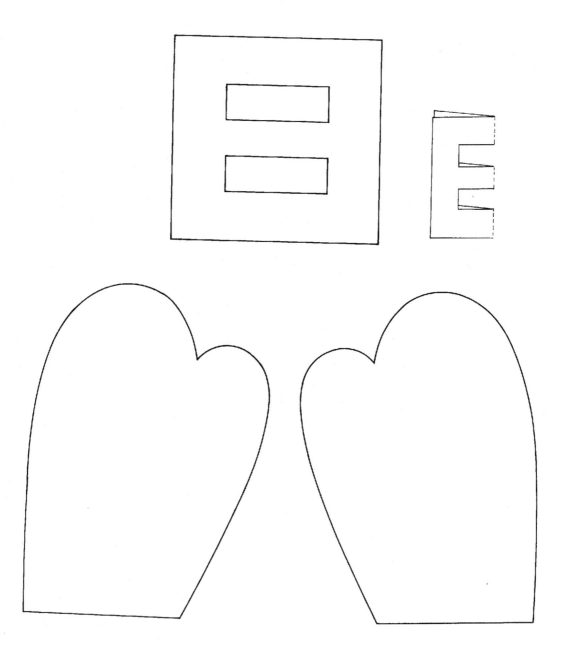

Santa Belt Buckle
Santa Mittens

Dreidel, Dreidel, Dreidel

General Objective:

Students will create a dreidel (spinning top) and then play the "Dreidel Game."

Materials and Preparation:

1. Provide a copy of page 83, the dreidel pattern, for each student and a copy of the score sheet found on page 85. (You need only one sheet for every two students.) If you have access to any real dreidels, they might be interesting for the students to see. They are usually made of either plastic or wood.

2. Purchase a one-pound bag of dried lima beans and provide calculators, one for every two students.

3. Ask each student to set aside 1 pencil approximately 7" long.

Activity:

Direct students to cut out the pattern on the heavy dark lines. They can color lightly or decorate the sheet, provided they can still see the letters. Instruct them to fold down the tabs and fold on the lines to form a cube. Next, have them paste or glue the tabs. (Students might need assistance with this step.) Carefully poke a short pencil through the center, as indicated, from top to bottom, so that the cube becomes a spinning top.

Ask students, "Why is this figure a cube and not a square?" Discuss the differences between two- and three-dimensional shapes.

When teaching students how to play the dreidel game, first explain what each letter on the dreidel means/stands for:

_____ is the Hebrew letter *nun* which stands for the word "nes," meaning *a miracle.*

_____ is the Hebrew letter *gimmel* which stands for the word "gadol," meaning *large or great.*

_____ is the Hebrew letter *hey* which stands for the word "haya," meaning *happened.*

_____ is the Hebrew letter *shin* which stands for the word "sham," meaning *there (in Israel).*

"A great miracle happened there" is a phrase which refers to the miracle of the oil that burned for eight days instead of one in the time of the Maccabees.

Pattern for Making a Dreidel

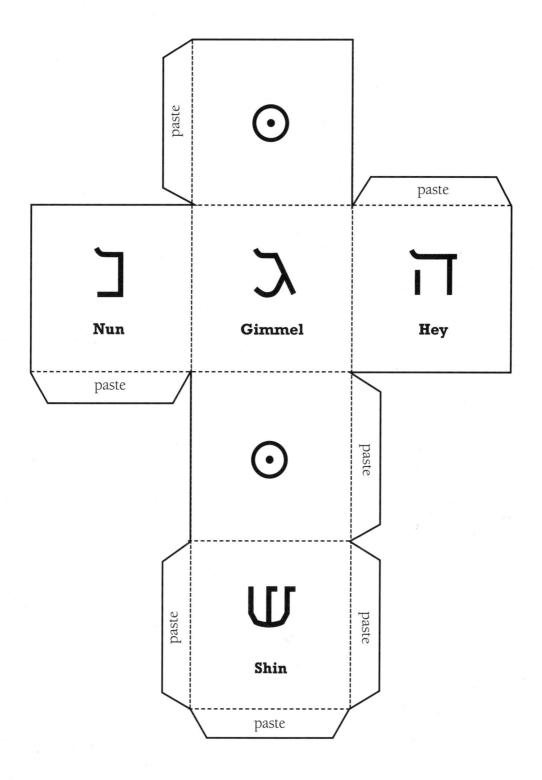

Playing the Dreidel Game

Divide students in the class into pairs. If there is an odd number of students in your class, you can have a threesome. Each student should get ten dried lima beans plus ten more for the center of the playing area or "bank." This makes a total of twenty beans, ten for the student and ten for each student to put in the center. Each group or pair of students should also have a dreidel game score sheet.

Each player spins his or her dreidel. The letter that is on top, or face up, when the dreidel stops, is the one they will read. If the top letter is nun, the player has to put one bean in the bank. If it is gimmel, the player gets all the beans in the bank. If it is hey, the player gets half the beans in the bank. (If there is an odd number of beans in the bank, the players can make a rule among themselves about how to handle such a situation.) If the facing letter is shin, the player must add the same number of beans from his/her pile that are already in the bank. For example, if there are five beans left in the bank and the player gets a shin, then the player puts five beans from his or her pile into the bank. When all of the beans in the bank are gone, the round is over.

Have students play five rounds, recording their respective scores on their sheets at the end of each round. They simply count the beans in their pile to obtain their score for each individual round. At the end of five rounds, each player adds his or her scores together to determine the grand total. They might need a calculator to do this. The player with the highest grand total is the winner.

TEACHER NOTE:

It is best not to roll a gimmel or a shin on the first turn because that will end the game. If that happens, the player should get another turn to spin so that the game can continue.

From *Writing Math: A Project-Based Approach*, published by GoodYear Books. Copyright © 1995 Sharon Z. Draznin

Score Sheet for Dreidel Game

(2 players)

PLAYER 1	**PLAYER 2**
Name	Name
Round One	
Round Two	
Round Three	
Round Four	
Round Five	
Grand Total	

Score Sheet for Dreidel Game

(3 players)

PLAYER 1	**PLAYER 2**	**PLAYER 3**
Name _____	Name _____	Name _____
Round One _____	_____	_____
Round Two _____	_____	_____
Round Three _____	_____	_____
Round Four _____	_____	_____
Round Five _____	_____	_____
Grand Total _____	_____	_____

From *Writing Math: A Project-Based Approach*, published by GoodYear Books. Copyright © 1995 Sharon Z. Draznin

DAY 6

Tree Of Cranes

Language Arts/Math Objective:

Students will listen to Allen Say's story *Tree of Cranes* (Houghton Mifflin, 1991) and then use origami to create their own paper birds. In the process of paper-folding, students will become more familiar with the mathematical concepts of one-half, diagonal, square, and triangle.

Materials and Preparation:

1. Obtain a copy of Allen Say's *Tree of Cranes* (Houghton Mifflin, 1991).

2. Prepare squares of various colors of construction paper—at least 1 per student.

Activity:

Read and discuss the book *Tree of Cranes,* which is about a Japanese boy who learns about Christmas when his mother decorates a pine tree with origami paper cranes.

TEACHER NOTE:

During this project, demonstrate each step and circulate among students to assist wherever necessary

1. Distribute a square of pre-cut construction paper to each student. Instruct them to fold the paper in half, diagonally.

2. Unfold it and identify the top and right sides of the square. Fold the top and right sides in so that they align with the diagonal crease. The paper should be shaped like a kite.

3. Fold the bottom (narrower end of the "kite") up to the wider top corner. Fold the narrow tip down to the straight edge.

4. Fold the entire figure in half, folding back from the middle. Pull the beak out. As the beak is pulled out, the neck moves up. Fold up the edges of the tail to make a triangle on each inside. The origami bird is completed! Students may draw in eyes and decorate their bird.

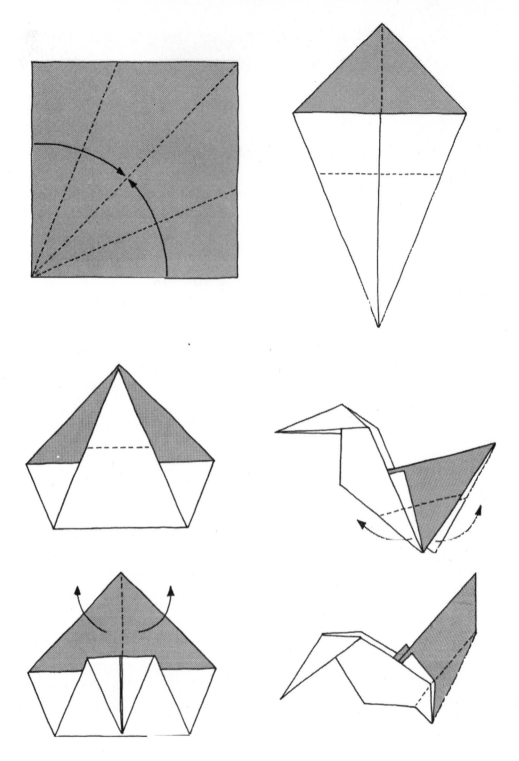

TEACHER NOTE:

Shapes can be identified and discussed as this project is being completed.

Extension:

A unit on cranes and/or birds could be taught using the activity from day six as an introduction to the unit.

From *Writing Math: A Project-Based Approach*, published by GoodYear Books. Copyright © 1995 Sharon Z. Draznin

DAY 7

Fun With Origami

with thanks to Diane Maier

INTRODUCTION:

The practice of paper folding goes back to the sixth century A.D. in Japan. The word origami means paper-folding in Japanese. It is derived from the word ori (folding) and kami or gami (paper). Kami can also mean God in Japanese. Originally origami was an expensive and precious skill which was reserved for religious leaders. It was spread by Buddhist monks from Japan to China, through Spain and to North and South America. Children today enjoy making sailboats, hats and airplanes out of paper. Paper-folding can help students develop fine motor coordination and eye-hand coordination, as well as enhance their listening and concentration skills. It's fun, has a mathematical (specifically geometric) basis, and helps develop visualization and problem solving skills.

Math Objective:

Students will create five objects using the technique of origami (Japanese paper folding) As they do so, they will discuss fractions and shapes.

Materials and Preparation:

You will need crayons, popsicle or paste sticks, scissors, straws, straight pins, and 4 or 5 pieces of paper (8" x 8") for each student.

Activity:

Establish five work stations in your room—one for each of the origami activities. Place a pile of 8" x 8" squares at each work station. You need to have enough to cover at least one sheet per student. You will also need to provide the volunteer for that station with a short training session and one model of the finished origami figure. Each work station is described below and includes directions for completing the designated object.

TEACHER NOTE:

The activities described below are easier to manage if you can get four parent volunteers to assist you; this way, each station has a supervisor. (See page 95 for Parent Letter).

Sailboat

1. Fold a square sheet in half diagonally.
2. Unfold it and fold the top and right sides in so that they align with the diagonal crease. The paper should be shaped like a kite.
3. Fold the remaining corner (the wide end of the kite) up so it touches the point where the two other corners meet.
4. Now fold the bottom (wide end) up again so the fold line is the line where the two corners meet.
5. Fold once more, making the top of the trapezoid in illustration four the fold line.

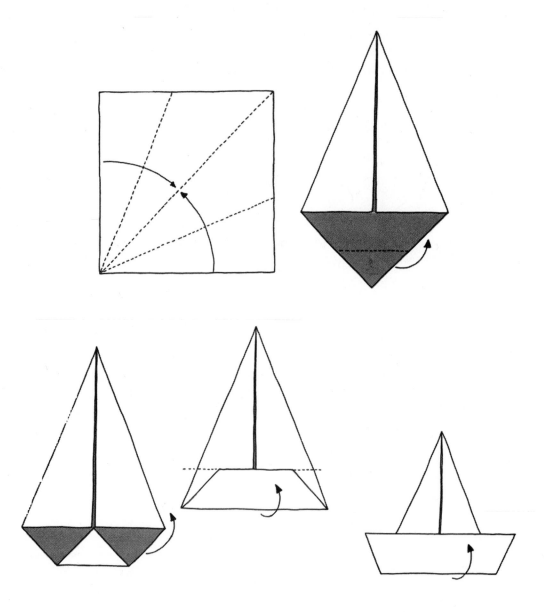

From *Writing Math: A Project-Based Approach*, published by GoodYear Books. Copyright © 1995 Sharon Z. Draznin.

Area Two:

Dog or Mountain With 3 Peaks

with gratitude to Diane Maier

1. Fold a square sheet in half, diagonally, forming a triangle. Draw a jagged line on the point opposite the fold to represent a snow covered peak. Draw a line down from the center of the "snow" to the bottom center of the fold line. Draw a small circle to the right of line. Color it in.

2. Fold up the two lower corners. Now the figure looks like this: a mountain with three peaks (figure A). If this figure is turned upside down and another eye drawn in, the figure becomes a dog (figure B). A popsicle or paste stick can be attached and this origami figure can become a puppet.

Figure A

Figure B

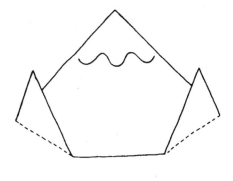

Whale

1. Fold a square sheet in half diagonally. Open it up and fold the two side corners to meet the center fold line (kite figure).
2. Fold the whole shape in half so that the folded pieces are on the outside.
3. The skinnier end is the tail, the wider end is the nose. Fold the tail up and fold the nose over.
4. Open the crease of the body and push the tail inside. Also push the nose inside. Fold the corners on the body near the head up to make small triangles (flippers).
5. Cut part way down the fold of the tail, about 1 1/4". Spread it and crease it to form the fins. Draw a mouth and an eye.

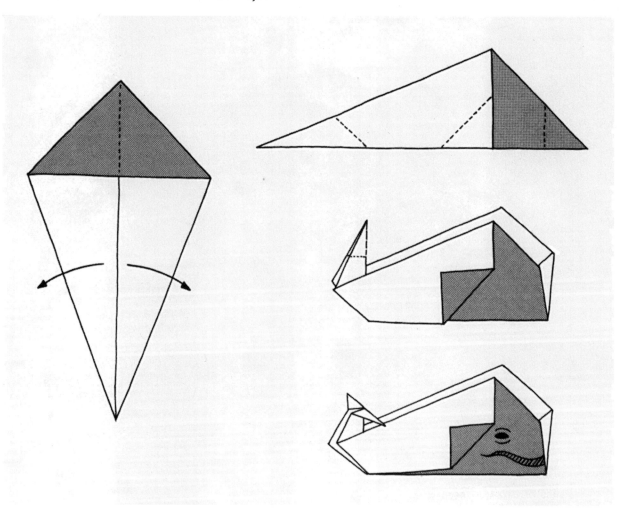

Fish

1. Fold a square sheet in half diagonally. Open it up and fold the two side corners to meet the center fold line (kite figure). Fold each corner of the wide part of the kite in to the center fold line (all 4 corners are now folded in, forming a narrow, diamond shaped figure).

2. Fold the wide points of the diamond (and the rest of each side) to the center fold.

3. Place the shape folded side down and fold in half on the original center fold line. Fold the tail up about 3" (the very narrow end). Unfold and carefully cut on the inner crease. Fold the tail up again. (It will be in two parts.) Draw eyes with crayons.

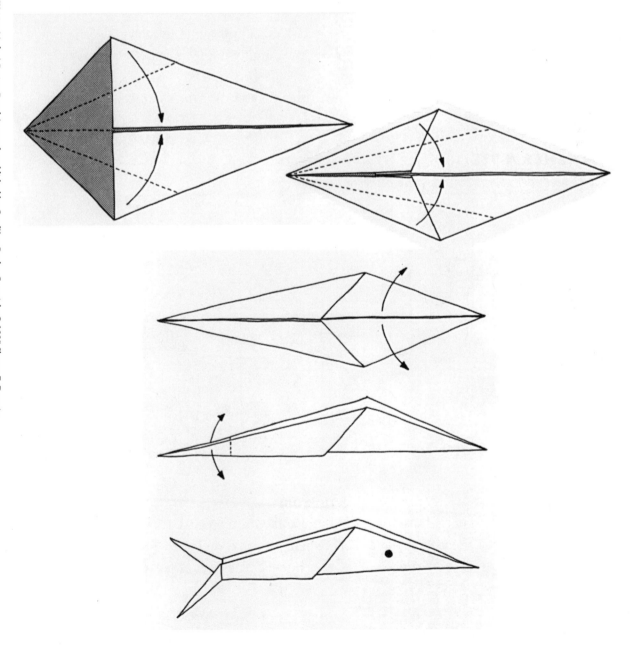

Pinwheel

1. Fold a square sheet in half diagonally. Fold it again on the opposite diagonal. Open and draw a circle in the center of the sheet (about 1 1/2" in diameter) where the two fold lines meet. Make an X in the center of the circle.

2. Cut in on each fold line, starting from the corner, and stopping at the edge of the drawn circle.

3. Fold in every other corner of each of the four sections (do not crease) and hold them down with your thumb. (Each section has two corners. Folding in alternating corners to the center will form the "fins" of the pinwheel which will catch the breeze and make the pinwheel spin.)

4. Carefully push a straight pin into the four corners and through the center X of the drawn in circle. Then push the pin into a straw. Adult volunteers may want to assist with this step.

5. Blow on the pinwheel and watch it spin! Push an eraser over the sharp end of the pin to prevent accidents.

TEACHER NOTE:

The outer edges of the pinwheel can be decorated.

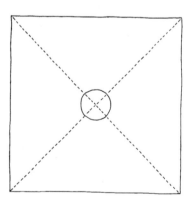 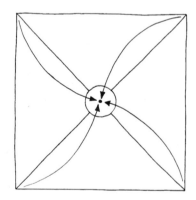 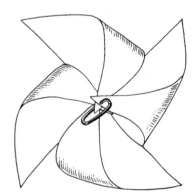

Extensions:

Students can choose their favorite origami figure and write a creative story about it. These activities can also be incorporated into a more extensive unit on Japan. Several students can do a research project on origami or another interesting aspect of Japanese culture.

Parent Letter

Dear Parents:

On _____ we will be making origami figures in math

class. Four volunteers are needed to assist me. One volunteer will be at each

work station. You will be given user-friendly instructions and plenty of sup-

plies. If you are able to give an hour of your time between _____

and _____please sign and return the bottom half of this note.

Thank you!

Sincerely,

Dear

I can help between _____ and _____

I will come to your room at that time.

Signed:

CHAPTER FIVE

Toothpicks and Marshmallows, Straws and Clay: Constructing Polygons

INTRODUCTION:

This chapter is about constructing shapes out of two types of materials: marshmallows and toothpicks or straws and clay. The mathematical focus of the activities is on geometry, i.e., identification and construction of both two- and three-dimensional shapes. The writing component activity entails composing a riddle about the shape beginning with the question: "Who Am I?" Students' riddle pages will be put together to make a class book. Another writing component of this chapter is called "Painting With Shapes and Words." Students will create a picture from shapes and then describe their picture—"painting with words."

DAY 1

Shapes and Riddles

....

Math Objective:

Students will construct polygons using a variety of materials.

Language Arts Objective:

Students will write "shape" riddles.

Materials and Preparation:

1. Purchase toothpicks, miniature marshmallows, bendable straws, scotch tape, clay, string and large-eyed needles.

2. Provide scissors for students. Reproduce the shapes on pages 101 to 106. Also reproduce the writing paper on page 29. Several sheets of the writing paper will be necessary for each student

Activity:

Identify, discuss and describe each shape found on the pages that you reproduced. The shapes are: square, circle, rectangle, ellipse, triangle, trapezoid, rhombus, parallelogram, octagon, hexagon, pentagon, and quadrangle. Tell students that they will be constructing these shapes, using one of three sets of materials: Toothpicks, and miniature marshmallows; straws and clay; or string (or tape) and straw. They will be able to cut the straws, if necessary.

Have the students choose their materials and work on their constructions.

TEACHER NOTE:

If bendable straws are used, one end of the straw can be slightly compressed and slipped into another end when creating shapes. Some students may wish to try to build three-dimensional shapes. In that case, you will also need to identify, discuss and describe a cube, rectangular prism, pyramids with both square and triangular bases, and a cylinder. (Other three-dimensional shapes may be too difficult to construct using the materials listed above.)

After students have constructed their figures, they will be ready to do the writing part of this activity. Demonstrate the activity first. Tell students that you will be giving them a riddle to solve. For example: I have four sides. All of my sides are equal. All of my angles are equal. Who am I? (I am a square.) Have the students give examples and invite them to call on classmates to elicit answers to the riddle. When you feel the students understand this activity, distribute the writing paper. Ask them to write their riddles down on the lined side of the paper. Then they will cut out the shape, using copies of pages 101 to 106 which you have provided, and paste it on the back of their written page. Students can then check each other's answers as they read each other's papers.

TEACHER NOTE:

These pages can be spiral-bound and made into a classroom book. Have students help create covers for both the front and back of the book.

From *Writing Math: A Project-Based Approach*, published by GoodYear Books. Copyright © 1995 Sharon Z. Draznin

Painting With Shapes and Words

Math Objective:

Students will create shapes pictures made out of geometric shapes.

Language Arts Objective:

Students will write "painting with words" essays.

Materials and Preparation:

1. Cut large (12" x 18") pieces of black construction paper into triangles, circles and squares, and leave some as rectangles. The shapes should be as large as the 12" x 18" paper allows because the pieces will be used as a background for the students' pictures.

2. Have the students cut out shapes which have been reproduced on various colors of construction paper. Do not use black for the smaller shapes because it won't show up well against the background. The shapes can be found on pages 101 to 106.

3. Prepare writing paper (page 29) for each student. After students have cut out the small shapes, place them in piles according to either color or shape. Place the large black background pieces in piles according to shape. Have all of these materials in an area accessible to the students, perhaps placed on a long table or countertop.

Activity:

Instruct students working in small groups to choose a large black piece of construction paper, perhaps their favorite shape. Have them choose some smaller, variously colored shapes as well. When they have chosen their materials, have the students create a picture using the large black piece of construction paper as the background and the smaller, colored shapes to form the picture. Tell them to place the shapes on their paper before pasting them down so they can be sure their picture is exactly the way they want it. Then instruct them to paste their shapes down.

Now that students have "painted with shapes," tell them they will be "painting with words." Discuss descriptive words (adjectives), listing them on the chalkboard as students give examples. Distribute writing paper. Ask students to include as many descriptive words as they can in the sentences they write to describe the shapes picture they have just created. Remind them about putting a capital letter at the beginning of each sentence and a period at the end of the sentence. Circulate and assist as needed during the writing time.

TEACHER NOTE:

These pictures and the accompanying descriptions would make an attractive bulletin board display.

From *Writing Math: A Project-Based Approach*, published by GoodYear Books. Copyright © 1995 Sharon Z. Draznin

Shapes

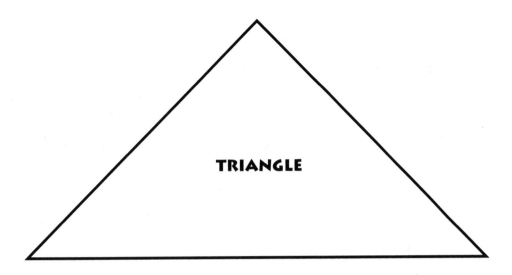

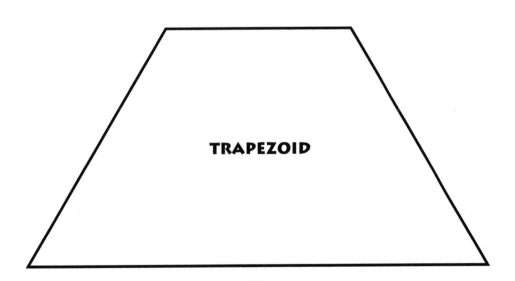

TEACHER NOTE:

Duplicate or xerox these shapes on colored construction paper (9" x 12" or 8 1/2" x 11").

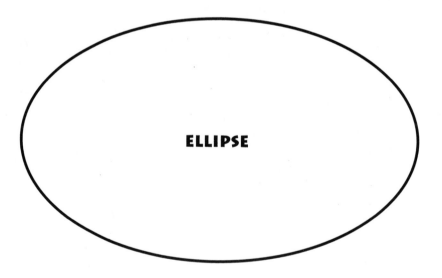

RECTANGLE

ELLIPSE

Shapes

SQUARE

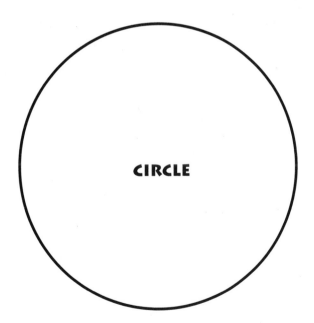

CIRCLE

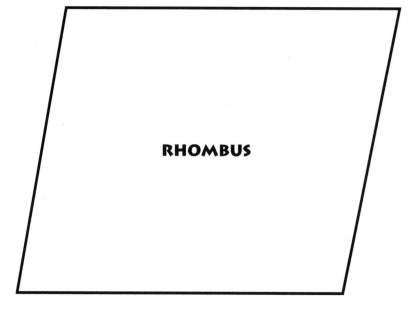

RHOMBUS

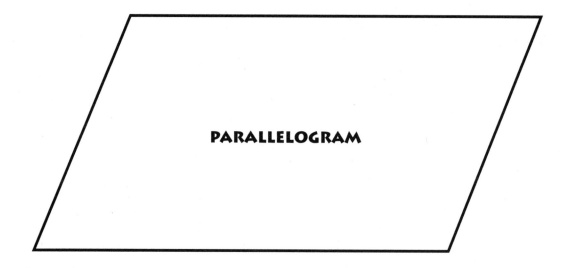

PARALLELOGRAM

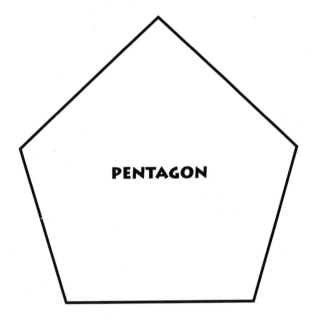

PENTAGON

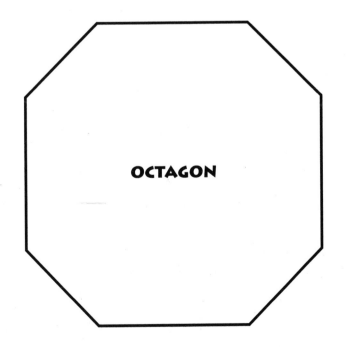

OCTAGON

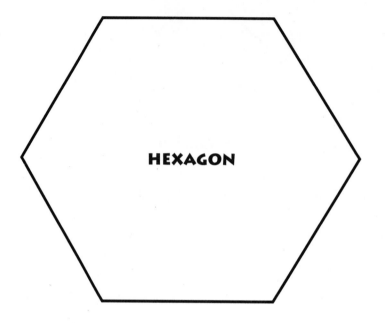

HEXAGON

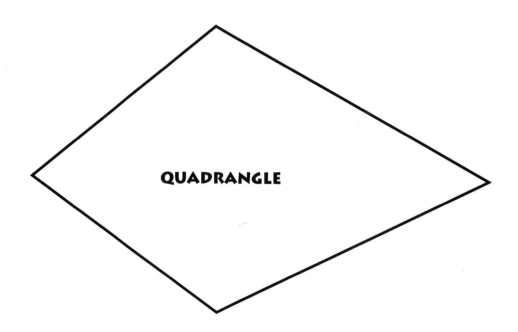

QUADRANGLE

From *Writing Math: A Project-Based Approach*, published by GoodYear Books. Copyright © 1995 Sharon Z. Draznin

DAY 3

Back to Building

Math Objective:

Students will build structures out of toothpicks and marshmallows, trying to make them as tall as possible. In the process, students will discuss shapes and estimation. They will use various measurement tools.

Language Arts Objective:

Students will write about their structure and describe the strategy they used to keep it from falling down.

Materials and Preparation:

1. Have students pair off. You will need colored toothpicks (approximately 50) and miniature marshmallows (approximately 20) per partnership.
2. Prepare copies of the "building record sheet" found on page 109, as well as the writing paper on page 29. If you have various measuring tools, such as a 6" ruler, 12" ruler, yardstick, meter stick, and a tape measure, have them available for student use.

Activity:

Explain to the students that they will be creating a building that will be strong and not fall down. Mention that objects are considered to be strong if they hold their shape and do not change when they are pushed or pulled. Have the students choose a partner. If you have an odd number of students in your class, you will have one threesome.

As you introduce the "Building Record Sheet," discuss the concept of estimation. Explain what the terms "educated guess" and "ball park number" mean. Explain that sometimes measurements and numbers must be exact and that at other times in other situations, numbers can be "guestimates." Quickly review the recording sheet, making sure students understand what to do and how to use the sheet. Also explain and demonstrate how to measure, beginning with the zero mark. If you have other measurement tools available, show them to the students. Discuss situations when you might use each one, asking questions such as: "When would it be appropriate to use a tape measure rather than a ruler?" Working with their partner, students create a structure that will not collapse. As they work together, they complete the "Building Record Sheet" which is provided. After completing their structure and record sheet, partners will write a narrative entitled, "How We Built Our Structure, What Shapes It Contains, and What Makes It Stand."

When students have completed their work, gather them together and have them present an oral report about what they have discovered, using their "Building Record Sheet" as the basis for their report. Ask students to share their written reports about how they built their structure, the various shapes it contains, and what they think makes it stand. [Give each pair a sheet of paper on which to write their names. Their structure will then be placed on this sheet and put in a display area.] At the end of this lesson, summarize what students have learned.

TEACHER NOTE:

After this lesson, it is suggested that the following book be read to the class as a follow-up activity.

Wilson, Forrest. *What It Feels Like to Be a Building.* Washington, DC: The Preservation Press, 1988.

Building Record Sheet

Names: _____

_____

1. Estimate how many toothpicks you will use in your building.

2. Estimate how many miniature marshmallows you will use in your building.

3. Estimate how tall your building is in inches and centimeters.

4. Draw your building here.

5. Count the number of toothpicks you used.

6. Count the number of miniature marshmallows you used. _____

7. Measure your building. How many inches tall is it? How many centimeters tall is it?

_____

8. What shapes can you see in your building?_____

9. What do you think made your building stand? _____

_____

From *Writing Math: A Project-Based Approach,* published by GoodYear Books. Copyright © 1995 Sharon Z. Draznin

From *Writing Math: A Project-Based Approach*, published by GoodYear Books. Copyright © 1995 Sharon Z. Draznin

DAY 4

Strongest Shape Stands

Math Objective:

Students will experiment with various geometric shapes to determine which shape is strongest.

Language Arts Objective:

Students will write a report (see page 113).

Materials and Preparation:

1. For every 2 or 3 students you will need five 3" x 5" cards, 2 rolls of clay, about 1" in diameter, 50 pennies or small counting chips, and a 4 oz. paper cup.
2. Prepare copies of the record sheet on page 112 and the "Strongest Shape Stands" report sheet on page 113 for each pair. Provide extra plain white paper for illustrations.

Activity:

Divide the class into partners (with one threesome, if necessary). Have students fold a

 3" x 5" card into three equal parts. Have them roll two lengths of clay into strips approximately 3" long and 1" in diameter. Distribute the record sheet to each pair of students. Have students support each folded card with two rolls of clay, one on either side of the card. Place the cup on the card. Using the record sheet, have students estimate how many pennies or plastic chips can be placed in the cup before the card collapses. Then have them do the experiment and record the actual number of pennies supported by the card prior to its collaps-

ing. (One partner can hold the cup very lightly on the card and one can place the pennies or chips in it, one by one.) Repeat these two steps, using an arched card between two rolls of clay instead of a folded card. Can anyone now answer the question at the bottom of the record sheet?

With their partners, invite students to experiment trying other shapes. When you think they've had sufficient time, ask them to share their conclusions with the entire group.

Next, have partners write a short report using the "Strongest Shape Stands" report sheet. Instruct them to describe what they did and what happened. Encourage them to illustrate their reports. Upon completing their reports and illustrations, have student pairs (or trios) share their work with the rest of their classmates.

Extension:

The two writing and reporting components of days three and four may not be completed on those particular days. You may want to have an extra day as a "catch-up" day, allowing time for students to complete both days' written and oral presentations.

Strongest Shape Stands

Names: _____

_____

_____

shape	estimate of pennies the card will hold up.	amount of pennies chips the card held up.
	My guess or estimate is _____ pennies or chips.	This shape supported _____ pennies or chips before it fell.
	My guess or estimate is _____ pennies or chips.	This shape supported _____ pennies or chips before it fell.

Question: Why are arches used to support tunnels?

_____

Extra: Try the same activities using other card shapes. What did you find out?

_____

_____

From *Writing Math: A Project-Based Approach*, published by GoodYear Books. Copyright © 1995 Sharon Z. Draznin

Strongest Shapes Stands Report

Names: _____

_____

_____

This is what we did: _____

_____

_____

_____

_____

This is what happened: _____

_____

_____

_____

How Close Can I Get?

Math Objective:

Students will explore the concept of estimation.

Materials and Preparation:

1. Purchase or make several large bags of popcorn. Also purchase small, brown, square-bottomed lunch bags.
2. Reproduce the "Popcorn Estimation" partner sheet which is found on page 115. You will need one for every two students.
3. Reproduce the individual "Popcorn Estimation" on page 116, one sheet per student.
4. Visit the library and check out the book by Frank Asch entitled *Popcorn*.

Activity:

Briefly review the concept of estimation with the students. (See Day 3 of Chapter Five). Explain to the group that they will be doing an estimation activity with popcorn. Remind them that they will need to keep their popcorn on their working surface, and to try not to get it on the floor. Have the students form pairs. Instruct them to fill a lunch bag with popcorn. Review the instruction for the "Popcorn Estimation" partner sheet.

After partners have completed this sheet, have each student pick up a copy of the "Popcorn Estimation" individual sheet and complete it. Any leftover popcorn can be eaten! After both the partner and individual activities have been completed, gather the group together in order to draw some conclusions.

Partner Sheet - Did each pair of students get the same amount of pieces? How were the original estimates close to the final amount counted or way off?

Individual Sheet - Did everyone's hand tracing contain the same number of pieces of popcorn? If not, why not? Were the original estimates "in the ball park?"

Ask students to share the reasons why they thought this activity was fun.

From *Writing Math: A Project-Based Approach*, published by GoodYear Books. Copyright © 1995 Sharon Z. Draznin

Popcorn Estimation
Partner or Group Sheet

Names: _____

_____

_____

Use popcorn to fill in the shape. Estimate how many pieces will be used. Then fill in the shape. Finally, count the pieces.

We estimated _____ pieces.

We counted _____ pieces.

This activity was fun to do because:

_____

_____

_____

From *Writing Math: A Project-Based Approach*, published by GoodYear Books. Copyright © 1995 Sharon Z. Draznin.

Popcorn Estimation
Individual Sheet

Name _____

Trace your hand here. Estimate how many pieces of popcorn will fit into your traced hand. Put in the pieces. Count them.

I estimated _____ pieces of popcorn.

I counted _____ pieces of popcorn.

This activity was fun to do because:

_____

_____

_____

CHAPTER SIX

Gung Hey Fat Choy or Happy Chinese New Year

INTRODUCTION:

The mathematical aim of this chapter is to familiarize students with counting by twelves using four-digit numbers. The written component of this chapter involves student reports on the animals represented in the complete cycle of the Chinese New Year.

The Chinese calendar is based on a twelve year cycle. Each new year is represented by a real or imaginary animal. The calendar includes the following animals: rat, ox, tiger, rabbit, dragon, snake, horse, sheep, monkey, rooster, dog and pig. The exact date for Chinese New

Year is different every year because the Chinese follow a lunar calendar, but it generally occurs in February. The celebration lasts for fifteen days and is the most important Chinese holiday.

Chinese New Year is a time for families and friends to join together. Families hope for happiness and good luck, which are symbolized by the color red. For this reason, children often receive coins wrapped in red paper as gifts. In preparation for the holiday, the house is thoroughly cleaned and great quantities of food are prepared. New clothing is purchased and gifts are exchanged. On the last day of the holiday celebration, a large parade is held with a dragon, the symbol of goodness and strength, as the central figure of the parade. This parade is called the Festival of Lanterns. Candles are placed along the length of the dragon which is made of wood and paper. As many as fifty men and boys carry the hundred foot long creature. As the dragon winds its way up and down the street, the candles bob up and down.

More detailed background information can be found in the Activities Bibliography on page 215.

DAY 1

Calendars Can Be Circles

Objective:

Students will create their own Chinese calendar or zodiac "wheels." In the process, they will be introduced to the concept "clockwise" and will gain experience counting using four-digit numbers (1984, 1985, etc).

Materials and Preparation:

Reproduce for each student the Chinese calendar which is found on pages 119 and 120.

Activity:

Distribute a Chinese calendar to each student. Demonstrate how to complete the sheet by continuing to fill in the years moving around the calendar in a clockwise direction.

TEACHER NOTE:

Explain the meaning of the word "clockwise" to students.

Review the instructions at the bottom of page 119. As students complete the sheets, circulate and assist them as necessary.

Chinese Calendar

Name _____

1. Color the animals on the next page.

From *Writing Math: A Project-Based Approach*, published by GoodYear Books. Copyright © 1995 Sharon Z. Draznin

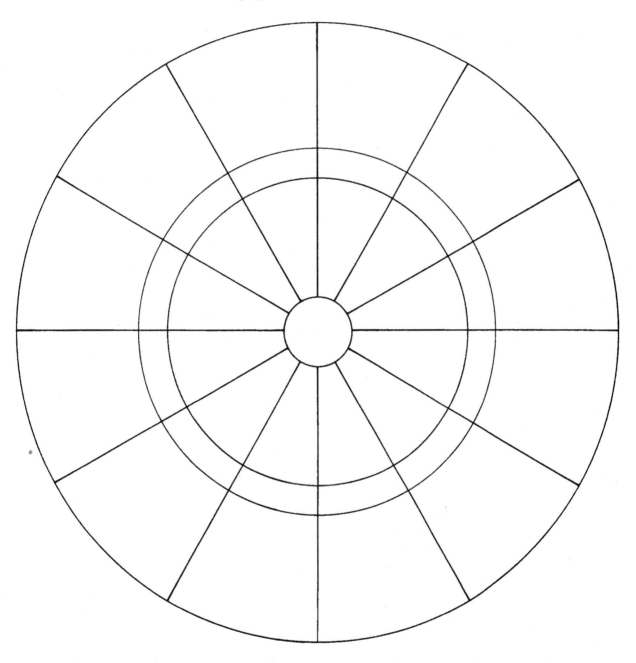

2. Cut out each one and paste it in the correct space by matching the name to the picture.
3. Continue filling in the years. The first two have been done for you.
4. What year is this year? It is the year of the _____.
5. What year will next year be? Next year will be the year of the _____.

Chinese Calendar Animals

From *Writing Math: A Project-Based Approach*, published by GoodYear Books. Copyright © 1995 Sharon Z. Draznin.

DAY 2

Counting By 12's

Objective:

Students will count forward and backward by 12's, beginning with the year of their favorite animal.

Materials and Preparation:

Reproduce copies of the Chinese New Year Record sheet found on pages 122-125, for each student. Have calculators available. Create a book display using books from the bibliography listed below.

Activity:

Give students some background information about Chinese New Year. Go over the directions for the Chinese New Year Record sheet. Ask students how they might figure out counting by 12's. If they can count by 10's already, forward and backward from any number, just adding or subtracting 2 more should be easy. Explain that calculators will be available but only to check their answers. They should try to figure out the 12-year cycle with their partner first.

Have students find partners. If you have an odd number of students in your class, you may have one threesome. Give each pair of students the Chinese New Year Record Sheets and go over the example carefully. Give other examples until you are sure students understand what to do. Then instruct students to begin. Circulate and assist them as necessary.

TEACHER NOTE:

If space is available, create a display or bulletin board of Chinese artifacts. Perhaps you or your students have objects to contribute such as fans, photos, books, etc.

Chinese New Year Record Sheet

YEAR		ANIMAL
1983		Pig
1984		Rat
1985		Ox
1986		Tiger
1987		Rabbit
1988		Dragon
1989		Snake
1990		Horse
1991		Sheep
1992		Monkey
1993		Rooster
1994		Dog

From *Writing Math: A Project-Based Approach*, published by GoodYear Books. Copyright © 1995 Sharon Z. Draznin

Chinese New Year Record Sheet

Example:

Choose the year 1987. Look on page one to see what animal goes with the year 1987.

1987 was the year of the

_____

When will the year of that animal come up again? HINT: If you add 12 years to 1987, you will find out.

$$\begin{array}{r} 1987 \\ +12 \\ \hline \end{array}$$

Now think again. What year was it before 1987 that was also the year of that same animal?

$$\begin{array}{r} 1987 \\ -12 \\ \hline \end{array}$$

Chinese New Year Record Sheet

Names:

_____

_____

Choose your favorite animal from the list on page 122. Figure out which years that animal will appear again. Then go "backwards" — figure out which years that animal previously appeared.

This is our favorite animal:

_____

Subtract 12 years

_____
_____
_____
_____
_____
_____

YEAR OF THE

_____

19_____

Add 12 years

_____
_____
_____
_____
_____
_____

From *Writing Math: A Project-Based Approach*, published by GoodYear Books. Copyright © 1995 Sharon Z. Draznin.

Chinese New Year Record Sheet

If you want to add more dates, use these sections. Cut out a section or both sections and paste the new section to the old one. Then continue adding and/ or subtracting.

cut in
half here ⟵

Our Favorite Animal

Language Arts Objective:

Students will do research and write a written report about their favorite animal from the Chinese New Year cycle.

Materials and Preparation:

Check out books from the school and/or community library and use them to create a display about the 12 animals that appear on the Chinese zodiac. Reproduce the pages of the "Our Animal Is A _____" booklet which can be found on pages 127 through 131. Make enough copies for each pair of students. Collate and staple the sheets at the top to create a booklet.

Activity:

Have students form pairs. Ask each pair to choose one animal on the Chinese zodiac. Explain to the students that they will be doing a research report on their animal using the materials you have made available to them. Discuss the concept of research with the students. Show them an example of a completed booklet. Go through it page by page, instructing the students about what information is needed to complete each page. Distribute booklets, circulate among students and assist them as necessary.

TEACHER NOTE:

This activity may take more than one day to complete. When all the students have finished their research reports, have a class sharing time, inviting pairs of students to share their reports with the entire class. You can also reproduce each report so that each student will be able to have a copy to take home.

From *Writing Math: A Project-Based Approach*, published by GoodYear Books. Copyright © 1995 Sharon Z. Draznin

OUR
ANIMAL IS A

_____

BY

Name: _____

Name: _____

This is what a _____ looks like.

This is what a _____ likes to eat.

This is where a _____ lives.

Here are some interesting facts about our animal, the

_____

Watch Out For The Dragon!

Language Arts/Math Objective:

Students will make a dragon puppet. They will create a repeating pattern on the dragon's body and discuss fraction of 1/3 and 1/2. Students will then write an imaginative story about their dragon puppet.

Materials and Preparation:

Copy the dragon puppet on pages 134-136, for each student. Copy page 134 on yellow construction paper, page 136 on red construction paper, and page 135 on green construction paper. Have an extra sheet of 9 x 12 yellow construction paper available for each student as well as a box of paper fasteners and a roll of tape.

Activity:

Distribute the pages for the dragon puppet and the extra sheet of yellow paper. Instruct students to fold the paper length-wise into thirds (step 1). Then fold the open ends to meet at the center (step 2). Fold the paper in half, keeping the open ends outside.

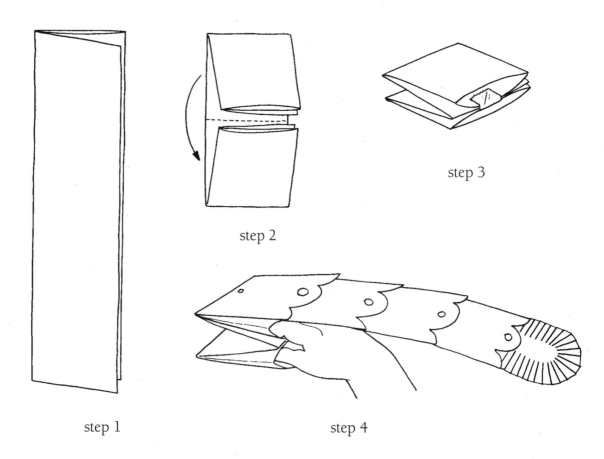

step 1   step 2   step 3   step 4

From *Writing Math: A Project-Based Approach*, published by GoodYear Books. Copyright © 1995 Sharon Z. Draznin

Distribute a small strip of tape to each student so they can tape the back of the mouth together. This procedure forms the dragon puppet's head (step 3).

TEACHER NOTE:

Discuss fractions of one third and one half as you instruct students to fold their paper.

Students will insert their hands into the open parts of the folded paper to make the dragon's mouth move. Use a paper fastener to join the head to the first tail section. Also use paper fasteners to connect the remaining two yellow tail sections and the one green section. In that way, the entire body and tail will move (step 4).

For the rest of the puppet, follow the directions on the dragon puppet sheet. The completed project should resemble illustration 5.

step 5

Next, distribute the dragon story paper on page 137. Encourage students to use their imaginations and creativity in naming their dragon and writing a story about the puppet. Elicit from students a vocabulary list which is to be written on the chalkboard.

Number each suggestion so that students can easily and quickly refer to this list when writing their stories. Words such as: fire-breathing, ferocious, large, and terrifying, might be used as "starters" if the students can't think of any words at first. As students write, remind them about using correct capitalization and punctuation as you circulate among them to offer assistance when needed.

When students have completed their stories, they can share them in a large group session.

Dragon Puppet

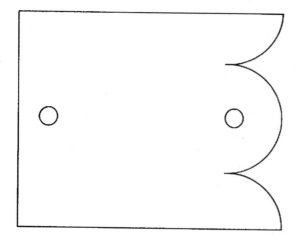

Note to the Teacher:
Reproduce this page on yellow construction paper.

Note to Students:
Cut out these shapes and create/draw a repeating pattern on each segment. Join the pieces together by using paper fasteners. Attach these to the head of the dragon puppet with a paper fastener.

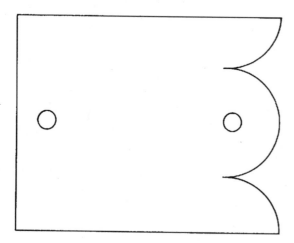

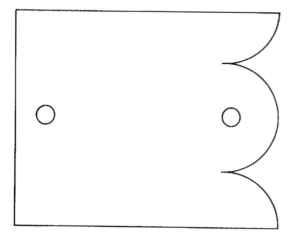

TEACHER NOTE:
Demonstrate to the students what you mean by a repeating pattern. Elicit from them a sample repeating pattern.

Dragon Puppet

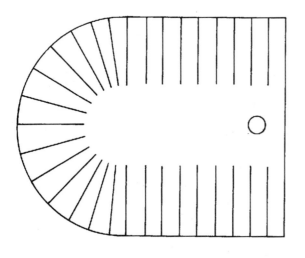

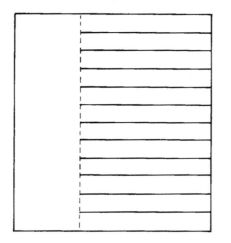

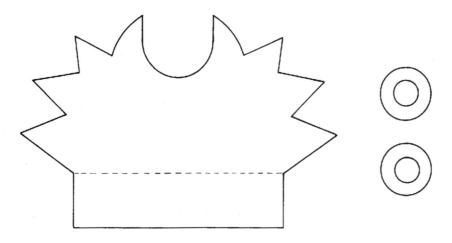

Note to the Teacher:
Reproduce this page on green construction paper.

Note to Students:
Cut out the tail section and fringe it. Attach the tail section to the last body section with a paper fastener. Curl the tail fringe around a pencil.

Next, cut out the horns piece. Fold and glue this piece to the head of the dragon. Now cut out the beard piece, fold it on the fold line and fringe it. Curl the fringe around a pencil. Glue it to the bottom lip of the dragon puppet's mouth.

Lastly, color in the centers of the eyes green. When this is done, cut the eyes out along the outer circle. Later the eyes will be glued on the red eye pieces.

Dragon Puppet

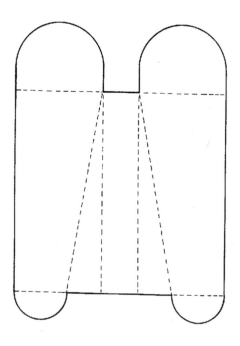

Note to the Teacher:

Reproduce this page on red construction paper.

Note to the Students:

Cut out the tongue. Glue the back of the tongue to the back of the dragon puppet's mouth.

After cutting out this last piece, fold it on the broken lines to form the bridge of the nose, the background of the eyes and nostrils. Glue this piece to the green horns and the top of the dragon puppet's mouth, as shown in the picture below. Glue the green eyeballs to the red background of the eyes.

TEACHER NOTE:

Complete this project as a total group lesson. Be sure to begin with the yellow sheet, followed by the green sheet, and concluding with the red sheet.

Name: _____

Title: _____

Name: _____

Title: _____

_____

_____

_____

_____

_____

_____

_____

_____

_____

_____

_____

_____

_____

From *Writing Math: A Project-Based Approach*, published by GoodYear Books. Copyright © 1995 Sharon Z. Draznin

Gung Hey Fat Choy Cakes—Happy Chinese New Year!

Math Objective:

While cooking "Happy New Year Cakes," a sweet treat for a sweet new year, students will apply fractions to a real-life situation.

Language Arts Objective:

Students will read a recipe and write a sequential story.

Materials and Preparation:

1. You will need double the amount of ingredients listed in the recipe on page 140.
2. Other materials you will need include: a large bowl, measuring spoons, a mixing spoon, waxed paper, a large deep pot or wok, a slotted spoon, paper towels, and a frying thermometer.
3. Reproduce enough copies of the recipe so that each student has one.
4. Also make one copy per student of "This Is How We Made Happy Chinese New Year Cakes," on page 143 and the dot-to-dot dragon on page 142.

Ask for parent volunteers to help. Make copies of the letter to parents on page 141 and have each student take one home.

TEACHER NOTE:

If feasible for your class, have the students bring ingredients and cooking utensils to school. Assign one ingredient or utensil to each student. Write an accompanying letter of explanation to parents with your request.

Activity:

Gather the students together and discuss the Chinese tradition of eating sweets for the new year in order to ensure a sweet new year. Explain the recipe and distribute copies to the students. Point out that in order to have enough cakes for each student, the recipe will need to be doubled. Talk about both the fractions and whole numbers in the recipe and how to double them. Write the doubled recipe next to the original on the chalkboard.

Gather students together around the cooking area. Make the cakes, allowing students to take turns adding ingredients, mixing, forming balls and rolling the balls in sesame seeds.

From *Writing Math: A Project-Based Approach*, published by GoodYear Books. Copyright © 1995 Sharon Z. Draznin.

TEACHER NOTE:

Make sure all students have washed their hands before beginning to cook. Have the parent volunteers assist you at this time. For safety reasons, parent volunteers should do the cooking.

While cakes are cooking, if there are any free moments, invite students to complete the dot-to-dot-dragon picture. Review counting by 10's, beginning with 10 and then using other numbers such as 12, 17, 31, etc. Instruct students to complete the sheet and color it. When the cakes are cooked and cooled, eat and enjoy!

Next, distribute the writing paper found on page 143. Invite the students to write a sequential story about how they made "Happy Chinese New Year Cakes." Review the steps with students, put the needed vocabulary words on the chalkboard (eg., mix, fry, roll, sesame seeds, etc.). Ask the students to mention at the end of their story how they liked the cakes. Include the reminder once again about using correct capitalization and punctuation when they write. Circulate and assist students as necessary. Hopefully, your parent volunteers will clean up! When students have completed their stories, they can be shared with classmates.

Bibliography: Use the Fractions Section of the Mathematics-Based Literature Bibliography.
Particularly appropriate is the book by Bruce McMillan entitled *Eating Fractions* (New York, NY: Scholastic, 1991).

Happy Chinese New Year Cakes

**This is the recipe we used for
Happy Chinese New Year Cakes.**

1 cup flour
1 teaspoon baking soda
1 teaspoon baking powder
1/4 cup sugar
1/4 cup water
oil for frying
sesame seeds

Mix the dry ingredients together in a bowl. Add water and mix well. Roll into 1 inch balls. Roll each ball in sesame seeds, coating each ball thoroughly. Place the balls on waxed paper and let them stand for 15 minutes.

Heat the oil to 360 degrees and fry the cakes until they are golden brown. Remove them from the oil with a slotted spoon. Drain them on paper towels. Once they are cooled, eat them and ENJOY!

(This recipe was doubled for our classroom.)

From *Writing Math: A Project-Based Approach*, published by GoodYear Books. Copyright © 1995 Sharon Z. Draznin

Parent Letter

From *Writing Math: A Project-Based Approach*, published by GoodYear Books. Copyright © 1995 Sharon Z. Draznin.

Dear Parents:

We have been learning about Chinese New Year. We plan to make "Happy Chinese New Year Cakes" on (date) _____ _____ from (time) _____ to _____ and we need some help. If you can come to Room _____ on the date and at the time listed above, please sign your name on the slip below. Return the bottom portion of this letter with your child. Thank you!

Sincerely,

(cut on the dotted line.)

Yes, I can help on (date) _____ from (time) _____ to _____ .

Signed,

From *Writing Math: A Project-Based Approach*, published by GoodYear Books. Copyright © 1995 Sharon Z. Draznin

This is how we made Happy Chinese New Year Cakes

by

_____

_____

_____

_____

_____

_____

_____

_____

_____

_____

_____

_____

From *Writing Math: A Project-Based Approach*, published by GoodYear Books. Copyright © 1995 Sharon Z. Draznin

CHAPTER SEVEN

Trash Bashing

INTRODUCTION:

Pollution, ozone, hazardous waste, acid rain, environmental wildlife protection, energy conservation—all are buzz words of contemporary times. This chapter focuses attention not only on math and language arts but also on attitudinal change. The major project  *described in "Trash Bashing" is designed to help students become more aware of how their actions directly affect the environment.*

Activities in this chapter are designed to make students more con of the amount of classroom trash that is discarded in one week (5 school days) and of how a more efficient use for at least a part of this trash can be found. Estimating, sorting, weighing and measuring activities are used to determine the volume of a week's accumulation of trash. Mathematical extensions (extrapolation) of the week's sample are made to provide estimates for a longer time period and for a larger group of samples.

TEACHER NOTE:

1) Since students may throw away less if they know the amount of trash they are discarding is being monitored, the trash should be collected for one week prior to telling the students about the project. Arrange for the custodian to assist in collecting trash.

2) Sorting and measurement (weighing) in this project will not be exact. This project aims at making an impact on students while providing them with practice using measurement skills, rather than exactness. Students will also need to decide if they will use the Standard System of measurement (ounces to pounds) or the Metric System of measurement (grams to kilograms). If they choose the Standard system of ounces, which is probable, help them to convert ounces to pounds to tons. Note: 16 ounces equals one pound; 2,000 pounds equals one ton. Students will need this information for the current lesson and the one following it.

"What Sorts Of Trash Do We Have?"

Math Objective:

After collecting ordinary classroom trash (excluding food materials) for a period of one week, students will sort, weigh, and graph the collection.

Materials and Preparation:

You will need plastic and/or paper grocery bags and a spring scale. Reproduce the Trash Bashing Record Sheet on page 149 for each group of students, and the Trash Graph on page 150 for each student. Prepare six 12 x 4 inch rectangles of white tagboard. Have a black marker handy, also.

Activity:

Collect classroom trash for a week (best done without students' knowledge) then present this project to the students. Tell them that they are going to sort, weigh and measure the trash. Divide the students into groups. Give each group a bag of trash to sort. Allow students to develop their own categories for the trash. Have the groups meet and combine their categories and trash. Direct this activity so that the goal is accomplished smoothly.

List the categories on the chalkboard. Possible categories could be: writing paper,

From *Writing Math: A Project-Based Approach*, published by GoodYear Books. Copyright © 1995 Sharon Z. Draznin

construction paper, pencil shavings, broken crayon pieces, paper plates, paper napkins, pencils, pieces of plastic objects, cardboard or corrugated paper, etc. Try to limit the categories to a manageable number. Ultimately, the group might settle on the following categories: paper, corrugated paper, pieces of crayons, plastic, and pencils. Shavings of any type may be too difficult to weigh. Miscellaneous items might all be combined into a category labeled 'Other.'

Ask students to estimate the number of plastic or paper grocery bags or fractions thereof needed for each category. Instruct students to fill bags to approximately the same level of "fullness." Have students return to their original small groups. Assign a category of trash to each group and have students fill bag/s with trash from that category. They will use sorted trash from each group's collection to do this. Have students count the bags, estimate how much they weigh and then actually weigh the bags in ounces and grams (if you have both types of scales available).

Write the name of each category of trash on a 12 x 4 inch strip of tagboard. Place each strip on the floor so that students will know where to place their bag of trash. Next, draw a bar graph on the chalkboard following the same categorical arrangement you have established with the tagboard strips on the floor. Have students line their bags on the floor behind the appropriate identification sign. As you draw the graph, explain to students that you are expressing in "picture" form what they expressed in their arrangement of trash bags on the floor. This "picture" is called a graph. Ask the following questions: "Which category has the most? Which has the least? Are there any ties? Why do you think _____ category has the largest amount? Why does _____ category have the smallest amount?" Distribute copies of the "Trash Graph" and have students copy the graph from the chalkboard onto their individual graphs. Compare the estimated amounts with the actual amounts of the various types of trash.

TEACHER NOTE:
Save the bags of trash. The trash will be used in subsequent days' activities.

Bibliography:
See the graphing section in the Mathematics-Based Literature bibliography.

Chalkboard Graph

6						
5						
4						
3						
2						
1						
	paper	**corrugated paper**	**pencil/ crayon pieces**	**plastic**		**other**

From *Writing Math: A Project-Based Approach*, published by GoodYear Books. Copyright © 1995 Sharon Z. Drazmin

Trash Bashing Record Sheet

1. These are the people in my group: _____,

_____, _____,

_____, _____,

2. This is our category of trash:

_____

3. We estimate that we will have _____
bags of trash.

4. We had _____ bags of trash.

5. We estimate our bag/s will weigh _____ oz.

_____ grams

6. Our bags weighed _____ oz.

_____ grams

Trash Bashing Graph

Name: _____

TYPES OF TRASH						Plastic	Food Waste	Paper	Cans, Tin	Cans, Aluminum	(number of pieces)
											2
											4
											6
											8
											10
											12
											14
											16
											18
											20
											22
											24
											26
											28
											30
											32
											34

From *Writing Math: A Project-Based Approach*, published by GoodYear Books. Copyright © 1995 Sharon Z. Draznin

DAY 2

Garbage, Garbage Everywhere

Math Objective:

Students will extrapolate information gained from the first day's activities. They will complete a sequential writing assignment.

Materials and Preparation:

Reproduce the 4 pages entitled, "Trash Bashing," "What We Did," "What We Found Out," and "What I Think About What We Found Out" on pages 153 through 156. Provide calculators for student use.

Activity:

Distribute calculators. Using the information gathered from the first day's activity, "What Sorts of Trash Do We Have," discuss the following questions:

1. What does the total amount of classroom trash for one week weigh?
2. How many weeks are there in the school year?
3. How many pounds of trash would there be for one classroom for one school year?
4. What mathematical operation/s did we use to figure this out?
5. How many classrooms are there in our school?
6. Assuming each classroom generates as much trash for one year as our classroom did, how much trash would the whole school generate?
7. Are there any re-useables in our trash?
8. If so, what ideas do you have for re-using these items?
9. Where does our trash go?
10. What do you think will happen to the trash if we run out of places to put it?

TEACHER NOTE:

Encourage students to use their calculators during this discussion. Leave the information that has been gathered as a result of this discussion on the chalkboard until the activity is completed. Students will want to use this information to complete their writing assignments.

Following this discussion, distribute the four reproduced pages previously mentioned. Demonstrate to students the manner in which these sheets should be completed. Direct them to write their name on the cover and draw what might be found inside the garbage can. Review the procedures from Day 1 and the conclusions that were reached during today's discussion, so that students can write pages one and two of their booklets. Page three requires student opinions. Invite several students to express their opinions orally to the group. This should serve as a stimulus to the other students and give them an idea of how they can complete the final page themselves. Remind students about using correct capitalization and punctuation. Circulate and assist students when necessary. When they have completed all four pages, staple them together to form a booklet. If time ,permits, share the contents of the booklets.

From *Writing Math: A Project-Based Approach*, published by GoodYear Books. Copyright © 1995 Sharon Z. Draznin

Trash Bashing

by

_____

Name: _____

This is what we did:

_____

_____

_____

_____

_____

_____

_____

_____

_____

_____

_____

_____

_____

_____

Name: _____

This is what we found out:

_____

_____

_____

_____

_____

_____

_____

_____

_____

_____

_____

_____

Name: _____

This is what I think about what we found out:

_____

_____

_____

_____

_____

_____

_____

_____

_____

_____

_____

_____

DAY 3

Can I Convince You?

Language Arts Objective:

Students will discuss how to reduce waste and try to think of as many ways as possible to do so. They will write persuasive letters in an effort to convince others to participate in recycling projects.

Materials and Preparation:

Make copies of the writing paper on page 29 and the information sheet entitled "Ten Ways to Reduce Trash" on page 158.

Activity:

By means of discussion, elicit from students and then list on the chalkboard their realistic strategies for reducing waste. Try to get as many plausible ideas as possible. (See the recycling bibliography at the end of this chapter.) Stress the idea that children can do some things to help with the recycling effort but adults also need to be influenced to actively participate in this effort. If your school does not yet have a recycling program, have your students write letters to the principal, trying to convince her/him to begin a school-wide recycling program. Instruct students to include in the letter reasons why recycling is important and some simple ideas that they think will work. If your school already participates in a recycling program, have students write persuasive letters to their parents trying to convince them to do more at home. Instruct students in following proper letter writing format by putting an example on the chalk board. Remind students about correct capitalization and punctuation. (This is an especially important component of letter writing.) Circulate and assist students whenever necessary. Invite them to share their letters with each other when they are finished. Distribute a copy of "Ten Ways to Reduce Trash" to each student and invite them to share this with their parents at home.

157

Ten Ways to Reduce Trash

Name: _____

1. Buy things that will last.

2. Buy things that come in recyclable, returnable or refillable containers.

3. Don't buy disposable items such as pens, diapers, razors, etc.

4. Don't buy packages that have lots of extra packaging materials.

5. Buy in large quantities, if possible. These packages use less packaging per ounce.

6. Participate in your community's recycling project.

7. Buy products that are packaged in recycled materials.

8. Use less paper. Try not to use paper plates, use scratch paper for notes, use cloth napkins and handkerchiefs.

9. Reuse whatever you can instead of throwing it out when you're finished with it. If you can no longer use it, take it to a garage sale, exchange it with a friend, or donate it to a charitable organization.

10. Try to influence others to reduce, reuse and recycle.

From *Writing Math: A Project-Based Approach*, published by GoodYear Books. Copyright © 1995 Sharon Z. Draznin

DAY 4

How Creative Can You Get?

Language Arts Objective:

Students will create 'junk sculptures' using trash materials gathered during the trash collection week prior to Day 1.

Materials and Preparation:

You will need the bags of trash collected during the week prior to Day 1, as well as old newspapers.

Activity:

Divide students into groups of four or five. Give each group some newspapers to spread out in their workspace. Distribute to each group some items from the previously collected trash. Instruct students to create a 'sculpture' or work of art out of their trash. Keep the trash accessible so groups can help themselves as they need more. Encourage groups to be creative. Ask students to name or give a title to their sculpture. Have them write the name of the sculpture on the bottom half of the card. The cards can then be folded in half and set in front of each group's sculpture. Share sculptures when all groups have completed their projects. Put them on display, either in your classroom or in a hall display.

TEACHER NOTE:

Each group can decide how they wish to present their sculpture—one large group sculpture or several individual sculptures with a common theme.

Sharing Trash Bashing in School

TEACHER NOTE:

Prior to today's lesson, have the class compose a letter to other classrooms, asking them if they would be interested in having a recycling box in their classroom. Reproduce copies of the letter and distribute it to other classrooms in your school. After receiving answers to the letter, determine how many boxes you will need. Ask the custodian to help you collect large boxes. If a large number of class rooms request recycling boxes, this activity may extend to more than one day.

Language Arts Objective:

Students will decorate large corrugated boxes with recycling symbols and slogans.

Materials and Preparation:

You will need a supply of poster paint, brushes, ecology/recycling stickers, if available, markers and a sufficient number of large corrugated boxes.

Activity:

Discuss the various symbols and slogans that could be used to decorate the recycling boxes. Illustrate them on the chalkboard. Divide students into groups of three, four, or five. Distribute drawing materials and allow sufficient time for students to complete their boxes. Assign student groups to distribute their boxes to the classrooms that requested them.

Extensions:

1. Invite a speaker from your local landfill or recycling center to speak to the class.

2. Plan a field trip to the local recycling center.

3. Ask students to keep track of trash collected at home for one week. Graph and discuss the results. Reproduce the "Home Trash Survey" on page 162 for each student as an at-home project.

4. Invite students to bring empty aluminum pop cans to school. Sell the cans to your local recycling center. Use the money earned to buy an acre of the rainforest.

5. Ask students to discuss "reduce, reuse, and recycle" at home, and to bring their ideas to school to share with their classmates.

6. Collect paper in school and use it to make recycled paper.

7. Plant a tree.

Home Trash Survey

Name: _____

TYPES OF TRASH							Plastic	Food Waste	Paper	Cans, Tin	Cans, Aluminum	(number of pieces)
												2
												4
												6
												8
												10
												12
												14
												16
												18
												20
												22
												24
												26
												28
												30
												32
												34

From *Writing Math: A Project-Based Approach*, published by GoodYear Books. Copyright © 1995 Sharon Z. Draznin

DAY 6

Trashless Lunch Day
(optional)

....

INTRODUCTION:

This day's activity is actually a whole school project which should be planned in advance. You will need the cooperation of the principal and the lunch staff. Lunch staff will probably need advance notice to prepare sack lunches for those students on free or reduced lunch.

Objective:

All students in the school will participate in a "trashless" brown bag lunch.

Materials and Preparation:

Reproduce the Note to Parents for a Trashless Lunch Day which is found on page 164.

Activity:

Students will bring lunch in a paper bag. The lunch will contain no throw-away packaging materials. After students have eaten their lunches, discuss the implications of a trashless lunch day. Was it really totally trashless? If not, why not? How were the concepts of reduce, reuse and recycle implemented? Could this activity have been improved in any way? If yes, in what ways could it have been improved? If no, what made it successful?

Trashless Lunch Day

Dear Parents:

In an effort to help students become more aware of the large amount of waste in our society, we are asking you to cooperate with us on (day) _____, 19____. We are planning a "Trashless Lunch Day" on that date. Please pack your child's lunch in a brown paper sack (which your child will be bringing back home to be reused.) On that day, please also use no throw-away packaging materials to wrap your child's lunch. Instead, use a reuseable/washable container for the sandwich, a reuseable jar or thermos for the drink, etc.

Thank you for your cooperation and remember, "reduce, reuse, and recycle!"

Sincerely,

_____

From *Writing Math: A Project-Based Approach*, published by GoodYear Books. Copyright © 1995 Sharon Z. Draznin

CHAPTER EIGHT
Growing Plants

INTRODUCTION:

This project consists of the process of planting and nurturing a flower bulb into a mature plant. Because of the time required for growing the bulb, the project will take longer than those in previous chapters to complete, even though each day's individual activity is relatively short. The plant's progress will be monitored by measuring its growth every other day (i.e., days 1,3 and 5). The writing component, a student journal, will be coordinated with the measurement activity. After the initial planting, you will need to provide short time periods for students to measure the plant and record its growth on the classroom and individual student graphs. You will also need to plan a 15-20 minute period for journal writing.

DAY 1

Planting A Bulb

Language Arts Objective:

Students will plant a flower bulb and then make regular entries in their journal, describing the process of planting the bulb, its growth, and its appearance when it has reached maturity.

Math Objective:

Students will graph the growth of the plant.

Materials and Preparation:

1. You will need old newspapers, a flower pot, soil, a flower bulb and water.
2. Select a bulb from the following possibilities: tulip, daffodil, Peruvian daffodil, amaryllis or gladiola.
3. Spread newspapers on the surface where you will be working. If possible, have a picture of the fully-grown plant available.
4. Make copies of the individual bulb growth graph found on page 167. Students can color in their graph with crayons in order to chart the growth of the bulb.
5. Prepare a large classroom graph. This graph should be exactly like the individual graph students are using. It would be useful to laminate the large classroom chart and use colored dots to chart the bulb's growth.
6. Make copies of each page of "My Bulb Growth Journal."

From *Writing Math: A Project-Based Approach*, published by GoodYear Books. Copyright © 1995 Sharon Z. Draznin

Activity:

Gather students around the planting area. Explain to them that they will be planting a flower bulb and that bulbs are members of the onion family. Elicit from them reasons why this might be so. Show the picture of what the plant will look like when it has grown to maturity and bloomed. Select volunteers to help put the soil in the planting container, to situate the bulb in the center of the pot, and to pat the remaining amount of soil around the bulb. Then select a student to water the plant. During the bulb's growth period, rotate the tasks of watering, measuring and marking the classroom graph with stick-on dots among students so that they all have an opportunity to be involved. For the first few days the plant should be placed in a dark location. After two or three days, relocate it to a sunny place. Distribute copies of "My Bulb Growth Journal" to the students. Have them complete the cover. After all students have done this, show them how to complete the first page. On this page students are asked to describe exactly how the bulb was planted. Elicit from students the steps that were involved and list these on the chalkboard in the correct sequence of their occurrence. Remind students just prior to writing in their journal to use correct capitalization and punctuation and to illustrate their journal entry.

From *Writing Math: A Project-Based Approach*, published by GoodYear Books. Copyright © 1995 Sharon Z. Draznin

My Bulb Growth Chart

Name: _____

inches of growth

	week one			week two			week three			week four			week five	
21"															
20"															
19"															
18"															
17"															
16"															
15"															
14"															
13"															
12"															
11"															
10"															
9"															
8"															
7"															
6"															
5"															
4"															
3"															
2"															
1"															
	1	3	5	1	3	5	1	3	5	1	3	5	1	3

My Bulb Growth Journal

by

_____

Name: _____

Date: _____

This is how we planted our bulb.

_____

_____

_____

_____

_____

_____

_____

_____

_____

Name: _____

Date: _____

This is how our bulb grew. This is how tall it is now.

_____

_____

_____

_____

_____

_____

_____

_____

_____

_____

_____

_____

Name: _____

Date: _____

Our bulb had bloomed! This is how tall it is now. This is what it looks like.

_____

_____

_____

_____

_____

_____

_____

Name: _____

Date: _____

I liked this project because:

_____

_____

_____

_____

_____

_____

_____

_____

_____

_____

_____

_____

DAY 2

(and until bulb blooms)

Measurement, Continued

Math Objective:

As the bulb matures, students will measure its growth in inches and graph its growth progress.

Language Arts Objective:

Students will continue to make entries in their Bulb Growth journals.

Materials and Preparation:

Provide a variety of measurement tools, such as a 6-inch ruler, a 12-inch ruler, a yardstick and a tape measure.

Activity:

Measure the growth of the bulb on days one, three and five of each week of this project and graph the growth on both the classroom graph and individual student graphs. In addition to this, students will enjoy estimating how much the plant will grow between measuring periods. That estimate can be written on the chalkboard and then compared to the actual measurement when it is taken.

Page two of the journal directs students to tell how the bulb grew. They should include the plant's measurement and describe its color, how many leaves it has and how much light and water it requires. When the bulb is in bloom, students can complete page three of their journals and then conclude the writing component with their personal opinion on page four.

During the journal writing and measurement period, there will come a time when a 6-inch ruler will no longer be useful because the bulb will have exceeded this length. See if students can tell you what to do about this problem. (Answer: use a longer measurement device, such as a 12 inch ruler.) Also, the plant may bend toward the light source. In that case, a straight-edged measurement device will not be accurate. Ask students how they might solve this problem. (Answer: use a tape measure.) This discussion can be extended to include the question of why we have a variety of measurement tools.

Bibliography:

See the sections on graphing and measurement in the Math-Based Literature Bibliography. A separate bibliography entitled Growing Plants is also included in the Activities Bibliography.

DAY 3

Flower Formations

Objective:

Students will learn to identify the parts of a flower.

TEACHER NOTE:

This activity should be done after the bulb has bloomed.

Materials and Preparation:

1. Make copies of "Identification of Plant Parts," parts 1 and 2 on pages 177 through 178 and the Plant Puzzle on page 179. Students should receive one copy of each. Staple parts 1 and 2 of the plant identification sheets together.

2. Prepare enough strips (15 inches long) of construction paper, in various colors to be distributed to each student. Use 12" x 18" sheets of construction paper to create the strips. Green, yellow, purple or pink would be good colors to use.

3. Have additional 12" x 18" sheets of construction paper of various colors available.

Activity:

Discuss and illustrate on the chalkboard the following parts of a flower: stem, leaves, petals, pistil, stamen, bulb or roots. Distribute the sheets entitled Identification of Plant Parts. Invite students to study the first sheet (part 1). Then have them complete part 2 without consulting page one. Assist them as needed.

Distribute the Plant Puzzle sheet and the 15-inch strips of construction paper. Instruct students to color, cut out and put together the "plant puzzle," gluing it onto the 1 5-inch construction paper strip. These strip flowers can be used to decorate a bulletin board.

Next, distribute the large pieces of construction paper and assign flower parts to various students. You will probably need two sets of papers since one flower variety can have as many as 16 parts (i.e., 1 stem, 4 leaves, 6 petals, 4 stamens, and one pistil). You can have another flower with 9 parts (i.e., 1 stem, 1 leaf, 4 petals, 2 stamen, and 1 pistil). Assign each student one flower part to draw. After students have drawn and cut out the large flower parts, have each group of students assigned to a part come forward as you name their part. Call the pistil first, then the stamen parts to surround the pistil. Next call the petals to stand alternately behind the stamen parts. Lastly, call the stem and the leaves. Invite each student to hold up his or her construction paper parts and you will have the two flowers!

Extensions:

1. Continue the study of plants by discussing the various uses of plants: food, clothing, shelter, oxygen, beauty, etc. Create a unit of study around these topics.

2. Study fruits, seeds, roots, stems and leaves. Discuss those we eat, those we plant, and the various sizes of these plant parts. Develop a classroom exhibit. Plan a snack which uses each part mentioned above.

3. Plant a classroom garden either indoors or outdoors. Care for it, watch it grow, and eat the "crops."

4. Study trees—various types, their parts and their uses. Arrange to visit a forest preserve.

5. Try some experiments with plants. Grow some with and without lights with various amounts of water, and in various growing media (i.e., soil, water, or sand). Record the results. What conclusions can be drawn?

From *Writing Math: A Project-Based Approach*, published by GoodYear Books. Copyright © 1995 Sharon Z. Draznin

Identification of Plant Parts

Part 1

Name: _____

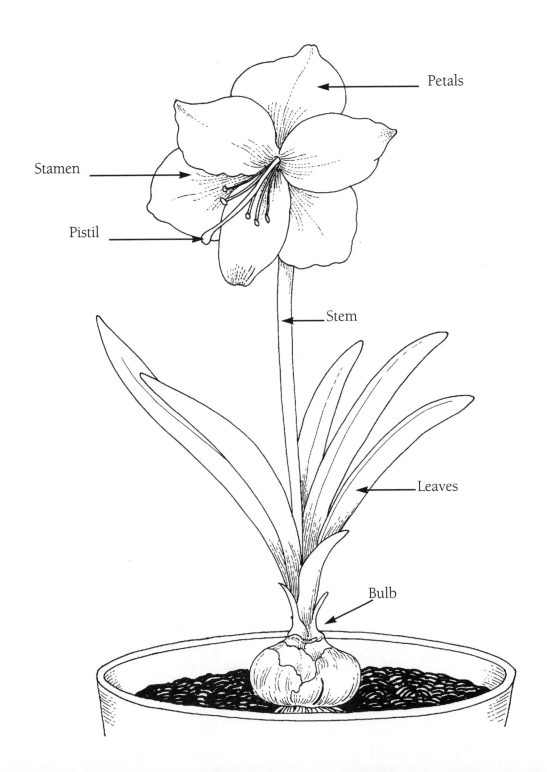

Identification of Plant Parts

Part 2

Name: _____

Plant Puzzle

Name: _____

Separate the pieces of the puzzle by cutting them on the dark lines. Color each piece.
Paste the pieces of the long sheet of paper that your teacher has given you. Make sure the
puzzle pieces are in the right order.

CHAPTER NINE

White Elephant Sale

INTRODUCTION:

The White Elephant Sale is an entire class project to be done in approximately a one-hour period. One half of the class will be buyers and the other half will be sellers (merchants). When half the allotted time has elapsed, the students will switch roles: the buyers will become sellers and the sellers will become buyers. The actual sale will take place on Day 5; Days 1-4 will prepare students for the sale.

This project is also interesting if you can cooperate with another classroom or two. In this way, the students can circulate between classrooms as they "shop." The mathematics skills in this chapter are identification and use of money, as well as making change. The written component involves sequential writing and composing advertisements.

DAY 1

What Is A White Elephant Sale, Anyway?

Objective:

Students will be introduced to the concept of a white elephant sale through story reading and discussion.

Materials and Preparation:

Reproduce the "White Elephant Sale" notice. Make sure you have enough to distribute one to each student with some extras. Provide a storage area where large items can be kept prior to the sale.

Activity:

Explain and discuss with the students the elements of the White Elephant Sale project. Tell them that they will be taking home a note explaining that they are to bring three toys and/or books which are no longer used. If students say that they have nothing at home to bring, tell them that they can make some things at home to sell. Examples of such items might be a bookmark, a decorated paper airplane, or a picture.

TEACHER NOTE:

On the day of the sale, have a few extra trinkets available such as stickers, toy cars, key chains, bookmarks, etc, for those students who do not bring in enough items. Also, it is a good idea to begin collecting plastic grocery bags for students to use as they "shop. " You might ask students to bring some from home.

Gather the students together in a group. Read a story to them from the White Elephant/Money section in the Activities bibliography, page 215. Also, you might consult the Using Money section in the Mathematics-Based Literature Bibliography.

From *Writing Math: A Project-Based Approach*, published by GoodYear Books. Copyright © 1995 Sharon Z. Draznin

The Primary Team is holding its annual

USED TOYS, BOOKS
AND
GAMES SALE

(date) _____ from _____ (time)

in our classrooms

To participate, a child must bring at least 3 used toys/books/games

and no more than 5 toys by _____ (date)

These toys will not be returned!

(A child may make items if no used toys, games, or books are available.)

Making And Filling Wallets

Objective:

Students will make "wallets" and practice counting money. They will cut out 2 dollars' worth of paper coins, which will be placed in the wallet. This "money" will be their spending money on the day of the sale.

Materials and Preparation:

Reproduce the coin sheets found on pages 186 and 187. If possible, reproduce the pennies sheet on brown construction paper and the other coin sheet on grey construction paper. Make one copy of each sheet for each student. For each student, make available a small white envelope 6 1/2" x 3 1/2" (normal letter size) and one large paper clip. Also, have on hand one real penny, nickel, dime and quarter for use with the whole class. You will also need one copy of the Business Permit on page 185.

Activity:

Distribute the envelopes, one to each child. Explain to the students that they will be decorating the envelopes since these will be their "wallets" during the White Elephant Sale. Instruct them to write their name, using a dark crayon, on the front of the envelope in large letters. Elicit suggestions from the students for appropriate designs and/or symbols. Put some of these on the chalkboard for reference. After students have completed their wallets, have them cut out two dollars' worth of coins.

Identify the coins with the students prior to cutting them out. Show them the actual coins as a basis of comparison. Discuss and illustrate on the chalkboard several ways of combining the available coins so that they add up to a dollar. Circulate and assist as necessary, making sure students have cut out only $2.00 in coins. Save the extra coins on their sheets for use on Day 3. Instruct the students to put their money into their "wallet" and not to seal it. Instead, give each student a large paper clip to use to secure the wallet so none of the money falls out.

Choose one student to decorate the border of the business permit. Choose another student to take the permit to the principal's office for validation with his or her signature.

TEACHER NOTE:

Prearrange this with your principal. Also, remind students to bring their White Elephants to class.

From *Writing Math: A Project-Based Approach*, published by GoodYear Books. Copyright © 1995 Sharon Z. Draznin

BUSINESS PERMIT

This is to certify that Room _____ has

been carefully inspected and is given official

permission to open and operate a business.

Signed,

_____
(Principal)

License Number_____

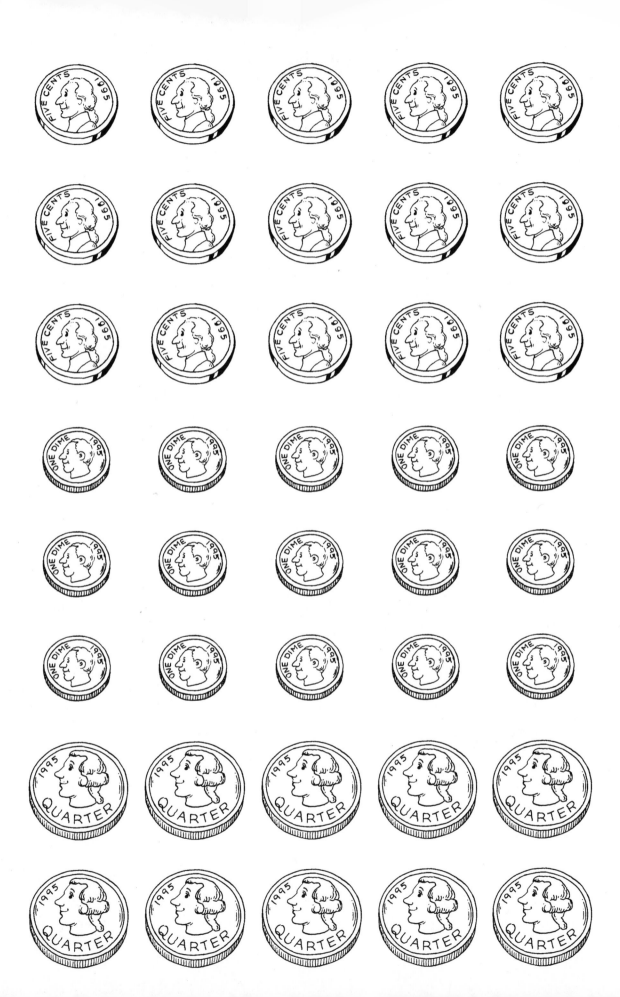

Making Change

Objective:

Students will practice making change and using various combinations of coins to create set amounts of money.

Materials and Preparation:

You will need the extra paper coins saved from Day 2. Make enough copies of "Practice Counting Money and Making Change" on page 189 so that you can give one copy to every two students, as well as "My Own Counting Money and Making Change" writing paper on page 190.

Activity:

Students will need to choose partners, or you might help them select partners. Distribute to each pair of students the sheet entitled, "Practice Making Change." Also make sure that each pair has a selection of left-over paper coins from the activity on Day 2. Demonstrate on the chalkboard several problems similar to those on the sheets. Ask for student volunteers to help solve the problems.

Instruct students to use the sheets and the coins to work out the problems. Circulate and assist them as needed. After a sufficient amount of time has elapsed and you feel most students have completed the activity, call on a pair to demonstrate each problem. There will be many ways to answer each problem.

When this activity is completed, distribute "My Own Counting Money and Making Change" writing paper. Invite students to create and write down their own problems, similar to those they have just completed. Remind them about correct punctuation and capitalization. Circulate and assist them as needed. Note that these problems can be compiled and made into a classroom book.

TEACHER NOTE:

Continue to remind students to bring their white elephants to school.

From *Writing Math: A Project-Based Approach*, published by GoodYear Books. Copyright © 1995 Sharon Z. Draznin.

Practice Counting Money and Making Change

Name: _____

Try these. Work with your partner. Use your construction paper coins to help.

1. I have some dimes, nickels and pennies. I want to buy a box of crayons for 27 cents. Which coins should I use?

_____

2. I have some quarters, dimes and nickels. I want to buy a box of watercolor paints for 40 cents. Which coins should I use?

_____

3. I have some quarters, dimes, nickels and pennies. I want to buy a notebook for 62 cents. Which coins should I use?

_____

4. I want to buy a marker that costs 17 cents. I give my friend a quarter. How much change will I get?

_____

5. I want to buy a pencil that costs 9 cents. I give my friend a quarter. How much change will I get?

_____

6. I want to buy a school supply box that costs 62 cents. I give my friend 3 quarters. How much change will I get?

_____

Now make up some problems of your own. Use the paper your teacher has for you.

From *Writing Math: A Project-Based Approach*, published by GoodYear Books. Copyright © 1995 Sharon Z. Draznin

My Own Counting Money and Making Change Problems

Name: _____

_____

_____

_____

_____

_____

_____

_____

_____

_____

_____

_____

_____

_____

DAY 4

Pricing White Elephants and More Practice Buying and Selling

Math Objective:

Students will price their white elephants. They will also continue practicing making change and buying items using various combinations of coins and objects from their school supply boxes.

Language Arts Objective:

Students will write advertisements to encourage their classmates to buy the items they have for sale.

Materials and Preparation:

You will need 1 package of white stick-on dots (at least 75 total in a package) to be used for pricing items. Each student should have his or her school supply box handy. Have extra construction paper coins available. Make copies of the "Ad Sheet" on page 193. You will need at least 3 copies per student.

From *Writing Math: A Project-Based Approach*, published by GoodYear Books. Copyright © 1995 Sharon Z. Draznin

TEACHER NOTE:

Some ads are started for the students that wish to use them. Other students may wish to use their own ideas. Provide them with plain writing paper.

Activity:

Distribute three white dots per student. Conduct a short class discussion in order to elicit appropriate prices. Instruct students to write the amount they decide is appropriate on the white dot and stick the dot to the item. Circulate and assist students as needed.

When all items are priced, have the students form pairs. Students should use objects from their school supply boxes as practice items. Have students practice making change as well as buying and selling using their extra construction paper coins. Again, circulate and assist as necessary.

TEACHER NOTE:

For this activity, you may want to pair students carefully, ensuring that less able students are paired with more able students so that peer tutoring can occur.

Distribute the "Ad Sheet." Tell students that they will be writing ads to try to get their classmates to purchase the white elephants they have brought to school. Discuss the purpose of advertising and elicit some examples of the types of ads students could write. Put some of these examples on the chalkboard. Also write down a vocabulary list of the names of students' white elephants on the chalkboard. Include words like "book," "toy," "game," etc. Remind students about using correct capitalization and punctuation. Circulate and assist them as necessary.

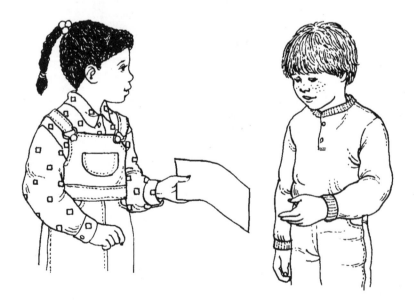

TEACHER NOTE:

These ads can be reproduced and cut in half so that students can hand them out to potential customers prior to the sale on Day 5.

Please buy the _____ I have for sale.

You should buy it because

_____

_____

_____

_____

_____

_____

_____

Signed _____

_____ for sale! It's a bargain,

only _____ cents. Buy it now, before it's too late!

Stop by _____ 's desk.

DAY 5

Sale Day!

Math Objective:

Students will buy and sell their white elephants.

Language Arts Objective:

They will write a sequential story about their experience.

TEACHER NOTE:

This activity is particularly interesting if two or more classrooms participate. In that way, students have a greater variety of items to choose from.

Materials and Preparation:

1. Divide the class as evenly as possible and determine which half will sell first and which will buy first. List the names on the chalkboard under the columns entitled "Sellers First" and "Buyers First."

2. Make sure students have both their "wallets" containing $2.00 in construction paper coins and their white elephants which are properly priced.

3. Distribute the plastic shopping bags to students.

4. Make sure that every student has at least 3 white elephants. If not, get out your personal "bag of trinkets" and distribute them accordingly.

5. Make copies of the "White Elephant Sale—How We Did It" on page 196 and distribute one copy to each student. Provide plain white writing paper for those students who need more than one page.

Activity:

Allow students a few minutes to distribute their ads to fellow classmates (see Day 4). Once this is done, announce to the shoppers that they may begin. Give them ten minutes or so in which to shop. During this time, circulate and assist students as necessary. At the end of the time period, ring a bell or turn off the lights and switch groups. (The shoppers become sellers and the sellers become shoppers.) Allow the activity to continue for an additional ten minutes. At the end of the second time period, gather the group together. Discuss how the sale went. Ask students to count their money. If there are students with

From *Writing Math: A Project-Based Approach*, published by GoodYear Books. Copyright © 1995 Sharon Z. Draznin

items that didn't get sold, conduct an auction. Explain what an auction is and try to have every student who has leftover white elephants dispose of them through the auction. After the auction, discuss the concept of profit and loss and the meaning of the term "net."

Have students fill out their copies of "The White Elephant Sale—How We Did It". Review with students the individual steps involved in this project. Write the key ideas on the chalkboard. Remind students about capitalization and punctuation. Circulate and assist them as they write their stories.

TEACHER NOTE:

These stories can be bound together into a classroom book and placed on your classroom library shelf. You can also include copies of the students' ads (see Day 4).

The White Elephant Sale — How We Did It

Name: _____

_____

_____

_____

_____

_____

_____

_____

_____

_____

_____

_____

_____

_____

CHAPTER TEN

Discovery Stations

INTRODUCTION:

The purpose of this chapter is to provide students with a variety of experiences using mathematics manipulatives commonly found in the classroom. The activities are designed to be structured yet also provide an opportunity for students to explore and discover on their own. The writing components of this chapter involve allowing students to describe what they discovered and also to have them relate what their favorite activity was and why it was their favorite.

The six stations are set up in advance in various parts of the classroom. Students are grouped and then each group rotates through the stations, two stations per day. The rotation process will take three days and the writing component two days, thereby taking approximately five days to complete the activities. The speed of rotation through the activities depends on the judgment of the teacher.

If all the necessary materials/manipulatives are not available in your classroom, perhaps you can borrow them from other teachers, from your public library, or from your local Educational Service Center.

DAYS 1, 2 & 3

Discovering Through Doing

DAYS 4 & 5

Discovering Through Writing

Math Objective:

Groups of students will use mathematics manipulatives in a variety of "real life" situations.

Language Arts Objective:

Students will write about their favorite activity and about what they discovered.

Materials and Preparation:

1. Make enough copies of the "Rotation Ticket" on page 201 to provide 1 for each student, as well as 1 copy each of the "Activity Sheet—One Through Six," the "Discovery Record Sheet" and "My Favorite Discovery Activity" sheets on pages 203 through 216.

2. Recruit parent volunteers in advance to assist at each station (see Note to Parents on page 200).

3. You will need: 1 set of attribute blocks, 1 set of base 10 blocks, 1 bucket of pattern blocks, pattern block templates, geoboards (5 or more) and rubber bands, scales (1 for ounces and 1 for grams), 2 sets of gram weights, a 6 inch ruler, 1 yardstick, 1 tape measure, calculators, 1 rock, various school supplies and books (as listed on the activity sheets), and a hole punch at each station for punching station tickets.

4. Make available 6 large containers in which to place each activity. Copy paper box tops work well.

5. Think about where you would like each station to be located in your classroom and place your stations accordingly.

6. Divide students into 6 groups (4 to 5 per group). Keep a list of each group and which station the group has visited. See teacher's worksheet entitled, "Groupings for Discovery Stations" on page 202.

7. Allow 20 to 30 minutes at each station. You will need 3 days to rotate through 6 stations, 2 stations per day.

From *Writing Math: A Project-Based Approach*, published by GoodYear Books. Copyright © 1995 Sharon Z. Draznin.

Activity:

Before beginning any activities, the following "rules" or guidelines should be discussed with the class.

Rules for Working Together

1. Treat the objects you are working with carefully.

2. Work quietly together; use "inside" voices.

3. Share materials.

4. If you have a problem, try to settle it in your group. If you can't, send one. person in your group to get help from an adult.

Explain and discuss the activity and record sheet to be completed at each station. Also, explain how the Rotation Ticket will be used. After each writing assignment, have the students share their experiences. Ask the students if any one else discovered the same thing or some other interesting idea they would like to share. Allow 2 days to complete the "Discovery Record Sheet" and "My Favorite Discovery Activity" sheet.

TEACHER NOTE:

For bibliographic information on base 10 blocks, see the Mathematics-Based Literature Bibliography sections "Large Numbers and Place Value" and "Numeration and Counting."

For attribute blocks, see sections on "Measurement" and "Attributes."

Also see the section "Geometry," which relates to the pattern block, attribute blocks, and geoboard discovery stations.

Request for help from Parents

Date_____

Dear Parents:

For the next three days we will be exploring several kinds of mathematics manipulatives. We need some help on those days so that participation in the activities at each station goes smoothly. If you can come to Room on any of the dates and at the time listed below, please sign and return the bottom part of this slip with your child. You will be given a station assignment and complete directions upon arrival. Thank you for your help and cooperation.

Sincerely,

_____

- -

Yes, I can help!

Day One _____

time _____

Day Two _____

time _____

Day Three _____

time _____

Signed _____

Discovery Station Rotation Ticket

Name: _____

1 Weighing	**2** Base 10 Blocks
4 Attribute Blocks	**3** Pattern Blocks
5 Geoboards	**6** Measurement

Groupings for Discovery Stations

Teacher's Worksheet

Group One

1.
2.
3.
4.
5

Activity One
Activity Two
Activity Three
Activity Four
Activity Five
Activity Six

Group Two

1.
2.
3.
4.
5.

Activity One
Activity Two
Activity Three
Activity Four
Activity Five
Activity Six

Group Three

1.
2.
3.
4.
5.

Activity One
Activity Two
Activity Three
Activity Four
Activity Five
Activity Six

Group Four

1.
2.
3.
4.
5.

Activity One
Activity Two
Activity Three
Activity Four
Activity Five
Activity Six

Group Five

1.
2.
3.
4.
5.

Activity One
Activity Two
Activity Three
Activity Four
Activity Five
Activity Six

Group Six

1.
2.
3.
5
5.

Activity One
Activity Two
Activity Three
Activity Four
Activity Five
Activity Six

Activity 1 – Weighing Objects

Name: _____

I weighed these objects: 1. a pencil, 2. a box of _____ crayons, 3. one rock, 4. a small bottle of glue, 5. a pair of scissors, 6. a book, and 7. (find an object of your own to weigh).

This is what they weighed in ounces and grams:

Ounces	**Grams**
1. _____	1. _____
2. _____	2. _____
3. _____	3. _____
4. _____	4. _____
5. _____	5. _____
6. _____	6. _____
7. _____	7. _____

Which object weighed the most? _____

Which object weighed the least? _____

Were there any ties? _____

From *Writing Math: A Project-Based Approach*, published by GoodYear Books. Copyright © 1995 Sharon Z. Draznin

Activity 2 – Base 10 Block Buildings

Name: _____

Build three "buildings" or structures. Count each one. What is each one worth?

Building One	**Building Two**	**Building Three**
I used:	I used:	I used:
_____ flats (100's)	_____ flats (100's)	_____ flats (100's)
_____ longs (10's)	_____ longs (10's)	_____ longs (10's)
_____ cubes (1's)	_____ cubes (1's)	_____ cubes (1's)
My whole structure was worth:	My whole structure was worth:	My whole structure was worth:
_____	_____	_____

Activity 3 – Pattern Block Designs

Name: _____

Make a beautiful design using the pattern blocks. Copy it here, using your template.

Activity 3 – Pattern Block Designs

Name: _____

Estimate the number of each pattern block shape you used in your design. Record it in the "Estimate" column. Tally first, then write the number. Finally add together the total number of pattern blocks you used. If you need to, use a calculator for help.

	Estimate	Tally	Number
☐ square	_____	_____	_____
△ triangle	_____	_____	_____
◇ tan rhombus	_____	_____	_____
◇ blue rhombus	_____	_____	_____
⬜ trapezoid	_____	_____	_____
⬡ hexagon	_____	_____	_____
Total	_____	_____	_____

My design had _____ pattern blocks in it.

From *Writing Math: A Project-Based Approach*, published by GoodYear Books. Copyright © 1995 Sharon Z. Draznin

Activity 4 – Attribute Block Sort

Name: _____

+--+
| **Vocabulary Box** |
| |
| 1. size   6. smooth   11. triangle   16. large |
| 2. shape   7. bumpy   12. circle   17. small |
| 3. color   8. red   13. square   18. thick |
| 4. thickness   9. blue   14. rectangle   19. thin |
| 5. texture   10. yellow   15. square |
+--+

Group the attribute blocks in at least three different ways. Tell how you grouped them. If you have time, group them in several different ways.

1. We grouped the attribute blocks by _____.

   We put all of the _____ ones together.

2. _____

   _____

   _____

3. _____

   _____

   _____

4. _____

   _____

   _____

5. _____

   _____

Name: _____

Create a design on your geoboard using rubber bands. Copy your design onto the dot paper. Can you make a design using only one shape? Try it and copy your "one-shape" design onto the dot paper.

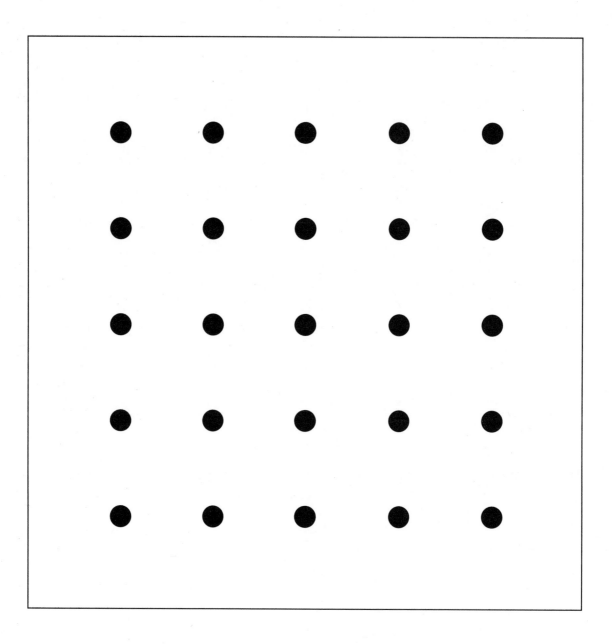

Geoboard Designs

Name: _____

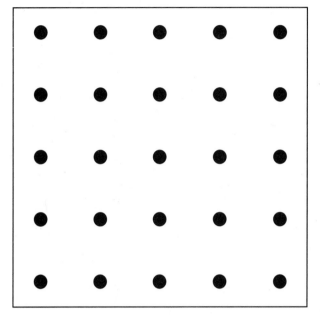
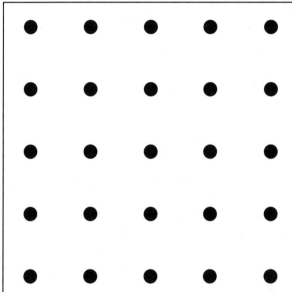
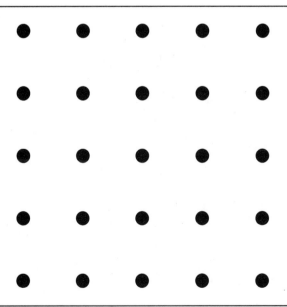
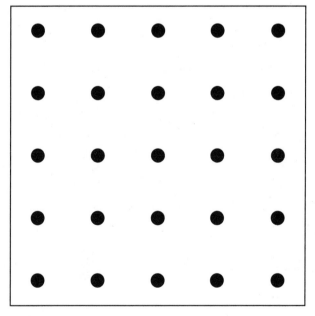

Geoboard Designs

Name: _____

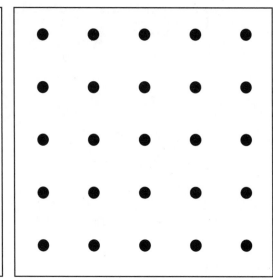
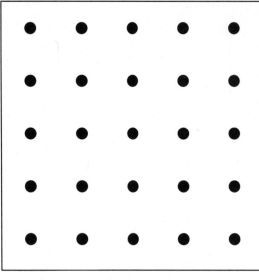

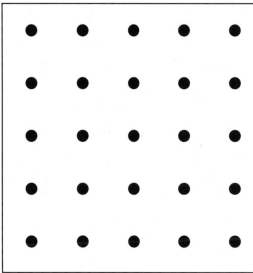
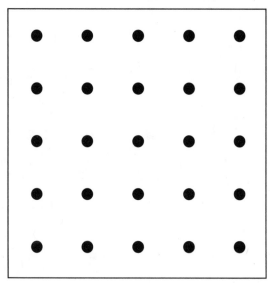

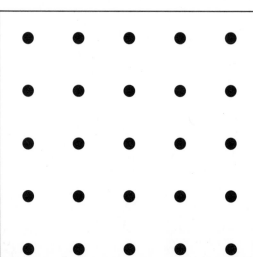

Activity 6 – Measurement

Name: _____

1. 6-inch ruler	4. tape measure
2. 12-inch ruler	5. inches
3. yardstick	6. centimeters

I measured . . .

1. A book:

    in.   cm.

length   _____ _____

width   _____ _____

I used a_____
to measure it.

2. My desk:

    in.   cm.

length   _____ _____

width   _____ _____

I used a_____
to measure it.

3. A large table:

    in.   cm.

length   _____ _____

width   _____ _____

I used a_____
to measure it.

4. The door to our classroom:

    in.   cm.

length   _____ _____

width   _____ _____

I used a_____
to measure it.

From *Writing Math: A Project-Based Approach*, published by GoodYear Books. Copyright © 1995 Sharon Z. Draznin

5. My school supply box:

             in.   cm.

length   _____ _____

width   _____ _____

I used a _____
to measure it.

6. Around my head:

             in.   cm.

length   _____ _____

width   _____ _____

I used a _____
to measure it.

7. Choose an object of your own to measure:

             in.   cm.

length   _____ _____

width   _____ _____

I used a _____ to measure it.

I chose this object because _____

_____

_____

_____

_____

Activity 7 – Discovery Record Sheet

Name: _____

This is what I discovered at:

Station One: Weighing objects. I discovered... _____

_____

_____

Station Two: Base 10 block buildings. I discovered... _____

_____

_____

Station Three: Pattern block designs. I discovered... _____

_____

_____

Station Four: Attribute block sort. I discovered... _____

_____

_____

Station Five: Geoboard designs. I discovered... _____

_____

_____

Station Six: Measurement. I discovered... _____

_____

_____

Activity 8 – My Favorite Discovery Activity

Name: _____

Vocabulary Box

1. scale
2. weighed
3. base ten blocks
4. structure
5. pattern blocks

6. template
7. calculator
8. attribute blocks
9. geoboards
10. rubberbands

11. shapes
12. ruler
13. yardstick
14. measured
15. length
16. width

My favorite activity was: _____

I liked it because: _____

_____

_____

_____

_____

_____

_____

_____

_____

ACTIVITIES BIBLIOGRAPHY

Apples

Aileen, Paul. *The Kid's Diet Cookbook.* New York, NY: Doubleday, 1980.

Dodd, Lynley. *The Apple Tree.* Milwaukee, WI: Stevens, 1985.

Gibbons, Gail. *The Seasons of Arnold's Apple Tree.* San Diego, CA: Harcourt Brace, 1984.

Grimm, Jacob. *Snow White.* New York, NY: Little, Brown, 1974.

Heuck, Sigrid. *Who Stole the Apples?* New York, NY: Knopf, dist. by Random House, 1986.

Hogrian, Nonny. *Apples: A Bushel of Fun and Facts.* New York, NY: Parents' Magazine Press, 1976.

Krementz, Jill. *The Fun of Cooking.* New York, NY: A.A. Knopf, 1985.

Le Sieg, Theo (Dr. Seuss). *Ten Apples Up On Top.* New York, NY: Beginner Books, 1961.

Lindbergh, Reeve. *The Legend of Johnny Appleseed.* New York, NY: Little, Brown, 1990.

Noble, Trinka Hakes. *Apple Tree Christmas.* New York, NY: Dial Books for Young Readers, 1984.

Ruben Patricia. *Apples to Zippers: An Alphabet Book.* New York, NY: Doubleday, 1976.

Scheer, Julian. *Rain Makes Applesauce.* New York, NY: Holiday House, 1964.

Schnieper, Claudia. *An Apple Tree Through the Year.* Minneapolis, MN: Carolrhoda Books, 1987.

Selsam, Millicent E. *The Apple and Other Fruits.* New York, NY: Morrow, 1973.

Watts, Barrie. *Apple Tree.* Morristown, NJ: Silver, Burdett Press, 1987.

Chinese New Year

Behrens, June. *Gung Hey Fat Choy = Happy New Year: Festivals and Holidays.* Chicago, IL: Children's Press, 1982.

Cheng, Hou-tien. *The Chinese New Year.* New York, NY: Holt, Rinehart & Winston, 1976.

Mahy, Margaret. *The Seven Chinese Brothers.* New York, NY: Scholastic, 1990.

Wallace, Ian. *Chin Chiang and the Dragon's Dance.* New York, NY: Atheneum, 1984.

Young, Ed. *Lon Po Po.* New York, NY: Putnam, 1989.

Christmas

Baum, Frank L. *The Life and Adventures of Santa Claus.* New York, NY: Dover, 1976.

Brown, Marc T. *Arthur's Christmas.* New York, NY: Little, Brown, 1984.

Gammell, Stephen. *Wake-Up-Bear—It's Christmas.* New York, NY: Lothrop, Lee, & Shepard, 1981

Hoff, Syd. *Santa's Moose.* New York, NY: Harper & Row, 1979.

Jones, Willis E. *The Santa Claus Book.* New York, NY: Walker, 1976.

From *Writing Math: A Project-Based Approach*, published by GoodYear Books. Copyright © 1995 Sharon Z. Drazmin

Wells, Rosemary. *Max's Christmas*. New York, NY: Dial Books for Young Readers, 1986.

Wild, Margaret. *Thank You, Santa*. New York, NY: Scholastic, 1992.

Cranes

Bang, Molly. *The Paper Crane*. New York, NY: Greenwillow, 1985.

Hyde, Dayton O. *Cranes in My Corral*. New York, NY: Dial, 1971.

Laurin, Anne. *Perfect Crane*. San Francisco, CA: Harper & Row, 1981.

McNulty, Faith. *Peeping in the Shell*. New York, NY: Harper Collins Childrens Books, 1986.

Roever, J.M. *The Whooping Crane*. New York, NY: Steck-Vaughn Co., 1971.

Roop, Peter and Connie. *Seasons of the Cranes*. New York, NY: Walker, 1989.

Dragons

Anderson, Wayne. *Dragon*. New York, NY: Green Tiger Press, 1992.

Baskin, Hosie. *A Book of Dragons*. New York, NY: Knopf, 1985.

Bertrand, Lynne. *One Day, Two Dragons*. New York, NY: C.N. Potter, 1992.

DePaola, Tomie. *The Knight and the Dragon*. New York, NY: Putnam, 1980.

Grahame, Kenneth. *The Reluctant Dragon*. New York, NY: Holt, Rinehart & Winston, 1983.

Krensky, Stephen. *The Dragon Circle*. New York, NY: Atheneum, 1977.

Lattimore, Deborah N. *The Dragon's Robe*. New York, NY: Harper & Row, 1990.

Mathews, Judith. *An Egg and Seven Socks*. New York, NY: HarperCollins, 1993.

Munsch, Robert N. *The Paper Bag Princess*. Toronto, Canada: Annick Press, 1980.

Williams, Jay. *Everyone Knows What a Dragon Looks Like*. New York, NY: Four Winds Press, 1976.

Wilson, Sarah. *Beware the Dragons*. New York, NY: Harper & Row, 1985.

Wrede, Patricia C. *Dealing With Dragons*. San Diego, CA: Harcourt, Brace, 1990.

Yep, Lawrence. *Dragon War*. New York, NY: HarperCollins, 1992.

Growing Plants

Bender, Lionel. *Plants*. New York, NY: Gloucester Press, 1988.

Budlong, Ware. *Experimenting With Seeds and Plants*. New York, NY: Putnam, 1970.

Carle, Eric. *The Tiny Seed*. Boston, MA: Picture Book Studio, 1970.

Gibbons, Gail. *From Seed to Plant*. New York, NY: Holiday House, 1991.

Heller Ruth. *The Reason for a Flower*. New York, NY: Putnam, 1983.

Pringle, Laurence P. *Being a Plant*. New York, NY: Crowell, 1983.

Webster, Vera R. *Plant Experiments*. Chicago, IL: Children's Press, 1982.

Weiner, Michael A. *Man's Useful Plants*. New York, NY: Macmillan, 1976.

Hanukkah

Adler, David. *A Picture Book of Hanukkah*. New York, NY: Scholastic, 1982.

Bearman, Jane. *The Eight Nights: A Chanukah Counting Book*. New York, NY: Union of American Hebrew Congregations, 1978.

From *Writing Math: A Project-Based Approach*, published by GoodYear Books. Copyright © 1995 Sharon Z. Draznin

Bial, Morrison D. *The Hanukkah Story.* New York, NY: Behrman House, 1952.

Burns, Marilyn. *The Hanukkah Book.* New York, NY: Four Winds Press, 1981.

Chaikin, Miriam. *Light Another Candle: The Story and Meaning of Hanukkah.* Boston, MA: Houghton Mifflin/Clarion Books, 1981.

Drucker, Malka. *Hanukkah: Eight Nights, Eight Lights.* New York, NY: Holiday House, 1980.

Kimmel, Eric A. *The Chanukkah Guest.* New York, NY: Scholastic, 1988.

Kuskin, Karla. *Great Miracle Happened There: A Chanukah Story.* New York, NY: Harper Collins Childrens Books, 1968.

Sussman, Betty. *Hanukkah: Eight Lights Around the World.* Morton Grove, IL: Albert Whitman, 1988.

Ziefert, Harriet. *What is Hanukkah?* New York, NY: Harper Festival, 1994.

Museums

"Beauty of a Feast; How a Museum Cooks Up a New Exhibit," *3, 2, 1 Contact,* April 1992: pp. 16-21.

Brown, Laurene Kransy, *Visiting the Art Museum.* New York, NY: Dutton, 1986.

"Is This Any Way to Tour a Museum? Kids Say Yes!," *World,* October 1990: pp. 9-13.

"The Museum," *Ladybug.* June 1992: pp. 20-23.

Weisgard, Leonard, *Treasures to See: A Museum Picture-Book.* San Diego, CA: Harcourt Brace, 1956.

Origami

Kallevig, Christine P. *Folding Stories: Storytelling & Origami Together As One.* Broadview Heights, OH: Storytime Ink International, 1991.

Lang, Robert J. *The Complete Book of Origami: Step by Step.* New York, NY: Dover, 1988.

Nakano, Dokuotei. *Easy Origami.* New York, NY: Viking Kestrel, 1985.

Randlett, Samuel. *The Best of Origami.* New York, NY: Dutton, 1963.

Poetry

Bauer, Caroline F. *Snowy Day.* Lippincott, 1986.

Cassedy, Sylvia. *In Your Own Words: A Beginner's Guide to Writing.* Crowell, 1990.

Cosman, Anna. *How to Read and Write Poetry.* New York, NY: Franklin Watts, 1979.

Ryan, Margaret. *Read and Write Poems.* New York, NY: Franklin Watts, 1991.

Recycling

Bailey, Donna. *What We Can Do About Litter.* New York, NY: Watts, 1991.

Foster, Joanna. *Cartons, Cans and Orange Peels: Where Does Your Garbage Go?* Boston, MA: Clarion, 1991.

Greenblatt, Rodney. *Aunt Ippy's Museum of Junk.* New York, NY: HarperCollins, 1991.

Hare, Tom. *Recycling.* New York, NY: Gloucester Press, 1991.

Lakin, Patricia. *Jet Black Pickup Truck.* New York, NY: Orchard, 1990.

Leedy, Loreen. *The Great Trash Bash.* New York, NY: Holiday, 1991.

Madden, Don. *The Wartville Wizard.* New York, NY: Macmillan, 1986.

Nardo, Don. *Recycling.* San Diego, CA: Lucent Books, 1992.

Seltzer, Meyer. *Here Comes The Recycling Truck!* Morton Grove, IL: A. Whitman, 1992.

Shanks, Ann Z. *About Garbage and Stuff.* New York, NY: Viking Press, 1973.

Silverstein, Alvin. *Recycling: Meeting the Challenge of the Trash Crisis.* New York, NY: Putman, 1992.

Simons, Robin. *Recyclopedia: Games, Science Equipment, and Crafts From Recycled Materials.* Boston, MA: Houghton Mifflin, 1976.

Stefoff, Rebecca. *Recycling.* New York, NY: Chelsea House, 1991.

Tusa, Tricia. *Stay Away From the Junkyard.* New York, NY: Macmillan, 1988.

Van Blaricam, Colleen. *Crafts From Recyclables.* Honesdale, PA: Boyds Mill/Bell Books, 1992.

Wilcox, Charlotte. *Trash!* Minneapolis, MN: Carolrhoda Books, 1988.

Riddles

Brown, Marc T. *What Do You Call a Dumb Bunny? And Other Rabbit Riddles.* New York, NY: Little, Brown, 1983

Calmenson, Stephanie. *What Am I? Very First Riddles.* San Francisco, CA: Harper & Row, 1989.

Cerf, Bennett. *Bennett Cerf's Book of Animal Riddles.* New York, NY: Random House, 1964.

Hall, Katy. *Buggy Riddles.* New York, NY: Dial Books for Young Readers, 1986.
    Grizzley Riddles. New York, NY: Dial Books for Young Readers, 1989.
    Spacey Riddles. New York, NY: Dial Books for Young Readers, 1992.
    Fishy Riddles. New York, NY: Dial Books for Young Readers, 1983.

Hoke, Helen. *Riddle Giggles.* New York, NY: Franklin Watts, 1975.

Maestro, Giulio. *Halloween Howls: Riddles That Are a Scream.* New York, NY: Dutton, 1983.
    Riddle Romp. Clarion, 1983.
    What's Mite Might?: Homophone Riddles to Boost Your Word Power. Boston, MA: Clarion, 1986.

Rees, Ennis. *Riddles, Riddles Everywhere.* New York, NY: Abelard-Schuman, 1964.

Using Money

Arnold, Oren. *Marvels of the U.S. Mint.* New York, NY: Abelard-Schuman, 1972

Cavin, Ruth. *A Matter of Money: What Do You Do With a Dollar?* Chatham. NY: S.G. Phillips, 1978.

Cribb, Joe. *Money.* New York, NY: Knopf, 1990.

Elkin, Benjamin. *Money.* Chicago, IL: Children's Press, 1983.

Fodor, R.V. *Nickels, Dimes and Dollars: How Currency Works.* New York, NY: Morrow, 1980.

Gross, Ruth B. *Money, Money, Money.* New York, NY: Scholastic, 1971.

Schwartz, David M. *If You Made a Million.* New York, NY: Lothrop, Lee & Shepard Books,

Wallace, David G. *Money Basics.* Englewood Cliffs, NJ: Prentice-Hall, 1984.

White Elephant/Money

Field, Rachel. *General Store.* New York, NY: Greenwillow Books, 1988.

Pearson, Tracey. *The Storekeeper.* New York, NY: Puffin, 1991.

Shelby, Anne. *We Keep a Store.* New York, NY: Orchard Books Watts, 1990.

MATHEMATICS-BASED LITERATURE GUIDE

The books in this guide were recommended by teachers who have used them to enrich their students' mathematics experience. They are intended primarily for grades K-3. This list is by no means comprehensive. You are encouraged to share your own recommendations and reviews in Teacher Link.

Special thanks to teachers Sharon Draznin (2nd grade, Washington School, Evanston, IL), Claire Hiller (1st grade, Orrington School, Evanston, IL), Beth Storey (kindergarten, Northside Christian School, Mounds View, MN), and Joan Stiber (kindergarten, Ralph M. Captain School, Clayton, MO) for their contributions to this guide.

Addition and Subtraction

Adams, Pam. *There Was an Old Lady Who Swallowed a Fly.* Boston, MA: Picture Book Studio, 1987.

Becker, John. *Seven Little Rabbits.* New York, NY: Scholastic Inc., 1991.

Carle, Eric. *Rooster's Off to See the World.* Boston, MA: Picture Book Studio, 1991.

Dunrea, Olivier. *Deep Down Underground.* New York, NY: Collier Macmillan, 1989.

Gerstein, Mordicai. *Roll Over.* New York, NY: Crown Publishers, 1988.

Gisler, David. *Addition Annie.* Chicago, IL: Children's Press, 1991.

Hawkins, Colin & Jacqui Hawkins. *There Was an Old Lady Who Swallowed a Fly.* New York, NY: G.P. Putnam, 1987.

Hawkins, Colin. *Take Away Monsters.* New York, NY: Putnam Publishing Group, 1984.

Hayes, Sara. *Nine Ducks Nine.* New York, NY: Lothrup, Lee & Shepard Books, 1990.

Hindley, Judy. *Mrs. Mary Malarky's Seven Cats.* New York, NY: Orchard Books, 1989.

Kherdian, David & Nonny Hogrogian. *The Cat's Midsummer Jamboree.* New York, NY: Philomel Books, 1990.

Krahn, Fernando. *The Family Minus.* New York, NY: Parents' Magazine Press, 1977.

Marshall, Ray & Korky Paul. *Pop-Up Numbers #1 Addition.* Los Angeles, CA: Price Stern, 1982. *Pop-Up Numbers #2 Subtraction.* Los Angeles, CA: Price Stern, 1982.

Rees, Mary. *Ten In A Bed.* New York, NY: Joy Street Books, 1988.

Schade, Susan & Joe Buller. *Hello! Hello!* New York, NY: S & S Trade, 1991.

Westcott, Nadine Bernard. *I Know An Old Lady Who Swallowed a Fly.* New York, NY: Little, Brown, 1980.

Attributes

Ahlberg, Janet & Allan Ahlberg. *The Baby's Catalogue.* New York, NY: Little, 1986.

From *Writing Math: A Project-Based Approach*, published by GoodYear Books. Copyright © 1995 Sharon Z. Draznin

Anno, Mitusmasa. *Anno's Aesop*. New York, NY: Orchard Books Watts, 1989.

    Anno's Flea Market. New York, NY: Philomel Books, 1990.

Dorros, Arthur. *Alligator Shoes*. New York, NY: Dutton, 1982.

Ehlert, Lois. *Color Farm*. New York, NY: Harper Collins Children's Books, 1990.

Fey, James. *Long, Short, High, Low, Thin, Wide*. New York, NY: Crowell, 1971.

Freeman, Don. *Corduroy*. New York, NY: Viking Children's Books, 1968.

Gelman, Rita G. *The Biggest Sandwich Ever*. New York, NY: Scholastic, 1980.

Handford, Martin. *Find Waldo Now*. New York, NY: Little, 1988.

Hoban, Tana. *Exactly the Opposite*. New York, NY: Greenwillow Books, 1990.

    Is it Red ? Is it Yellow? Is it Blue? New York, NY: Greenwillow Books, 1990.

    Of Colors and Things. New York, NY: Greenwillow Books, 1989.

Hoberman, Mary Ann. *A House is a House For Me*. New York, NY: Puffin Books, 1993.

Kroll, Steven. *The Biggest Pumpkin Ever*. New York, NY: Scholastic, 1984.

Lexau, Joan M. *The Big, Big Pumpkin*. Middletown, CT: Weekly Reader Books, 1985.

Lobel, Arnold. *Frog and Toad Are Friends*. New York, NY: Harper Collins Children's Books, 1970.

Ockenga, Starr. *World of Wonders, A Trip Through Numbers*. Boston, MA: Houghton Mifflin, 1988.

Parnall, Peter. *Feet!* New York, NY: Macmillan Children's Group, 1988.

Reid, Margarette S. *The Button Box*. New York, NY: Dutton Children's Books, 1990.

Schwanger, Istar. *Sorting*. Lincolnwood, IL: Publications International Ltd., 1993.

    What's Different? Lincolnwood, IL: Publications International Ltd., 1993.

Spier, Peter. *CRASH! BANG! BOOM!* New York, NY: Doubleday, 1990.

    People. New York, NY: Doubleday, 1988.

Young, Ed. *Seven Blind Mice*. New York, NY: Scholastic, 1992.

Estimation

Aardema, Verna. *Bringing the Rain to Kapiti Plain*. New York, NY: Dial Books for Young Readers, 1981.

Adler, David. *Base Five*. New York, NY: Crowell, 1975.

    Roman Numerals. New York, NY: Harper Collins Children's Books, 1977.

Anno, Mitsumasa. *Anno's Counting House*. New York, NY: Philomel Books, 1982.

Asch, Frank. *Popcorn*. New York, NY: Putnam, 1990.

Asimov, Isaac. *How Did We Find Out About Numbers?* New York, NY: Walker & Co., 1973.

Caroll, Lewis. *The Walrus and the Carpener*. New York, NY: H. Holt & Co., 1990.

Charosh, Mannis. *Number Ideas Through Pictures*. New York, NY: Crowell, 1974.

Clark, Ann Nolan. *Tia Maria's Garden*. New York, NY: Viking Press, 1963.

dePaola, Tomie. *Pancakes for Breakfast*. San Diego, CA: Harcourt Brace, 1978.

Froman, Robert. *Less Than Nothing Is Really Something*. New York, NY: Crowell, 1973.

Gantschev, Ivan. *The Train to Grandma's*. Boston, MA: Picture Book Studio, 1991.

Hoban, Tana. *Count and See*. New York, NY: Macmillan Children's Group, 1972.

Hutchins, Pat. *One Hunter*. New York, NY: Greenwillow Books, 1982.

Kaufman, Joe. *Big and Little.* Auburn, ME: Ladybird Books, 1992.

Keats, Ezra Jack. *Apartment Three.* New York, NY: Macmillan Children's Group, 1986.

Krensky, Stephen. *Big Time Bears.* New York, NY: Little, 1989.

Linn, Charles F. *Estimation.* New York, NY: Crowell, 1970.

Lobel, Arnold. *Ming Lo Moves The Mountain.* New York, NY: Greenwillow Books, 1982.

Martin, Jr., Bill. *The Happy Hippopotami.* San Diego, CA: Harcourt Brace, 1991.

McGraw, Sheila & Paul Cline. *My Mother's Hands.* San Diego, CA: Medlicott Press, 1991.

McKissack, Patricia. *A Million Fish . . . More or Less.* New York, NY: Knopf Books for Young Readers, 1992.

Munsch, Robert. *Something Good.* Buffalo, NY: Firefly Books, 1990.

Parker, Tom. *In One Day.* Boston, MA: Houghton Mifflin, 1984.

Rankin, Laura. *The Handmade Alphabet.* New York, NY: Dial Books for Young Readers, 1991

Schenk deRegniers, Beatrice. *So Many Cats.* Boston, MA: Clarion Books, 1985.

Sharmat, Marjorie Weinman. *The 329th Friend.* New York, NY: Macmillan Children's Group, 1992.

Shaw, Charles. *It Looked Like Spilt Milk.* New York, NY: Harper Collins Children's Books, 1988.

Simon, Leonard & Jeanne Benedict. *The Day the Numbers Disappeared.* New York, NY: Whittlesey - McGraw, 1963.

Tolstoi, Alexie. *The Great Big Enormous Turnip.* New York, NY: Orchard Books Watts, 1968.

Turkle, Brinton. *Do Not Open.* New York, NY: Puffin Books, 1993.

Ueno, Noriko. *Elephant Buttons.* San Francisco, CA: Harper & Row, 1973.

Walsh, Ellen Stoll. *Mouse Count.* San Diego, CA: Harcourt Brace, 1991.

Fractions

Dennis, J. Richard. *Fractions Are Parts of Things.* New York, NY: Harper Collins Children's Books, 1972.

Froman, Robert. *Angles Are As Easy As Pie.* New York, NY: Crowell, 1975.

Matthews, Louise. *Gator Pie.* New York, NY: Dodd, Mead, 1979.

McMillan, Bruce. *Eating Fractions.* New York, NY: Scholastic, 1992.

Moncure, Jane Belk. *How Many Ways Can You Cut a Pie?* Plymouth, MN: Child's World, 1993.

Shelby, Anne. *Potluck.* New York, NY: Orchard Books Watts, 1994.

Silverstein, Shel. *A Giraffe and a Half.* New York, NY: Harper Collins Children's Books, 1964.

Geometry

Adler, David. *3D, 2D, lD.* New York, NY: Crowell, 1975.

Birch, David. *The King's Chessboard.* New York, NY: Dial Books for Young Readers, 1988.

Birmingham, Duncan. *"M" is for Mirror.* New York, NY: Park West Publications, 1989.

Budney, B. *A Kiss is Round: Verses.* New York, NY: Lothrop, Lee & Shepard Co., 1954.

Carle, Eric. *My Very First Book of Shapes.* New York, NY: Harper Collins Children's Books, 1985.

From *Writing Math: A Project-Based Approach*, published by GoodYear Books. Copyright © 1995 Sharon Z. Draznin

  The Secret Birthday Message. New York, NY: Harper Collins Children's Books, 1986.

Charles, N.N. *What Am I? Looking Through Shapes at Apples and Grapes.* New York, NY: Blue Sky Press, 1994.

Charosh, Mannis. *Straight Lines, Parallel Lines, Perpendicular Lines.* New York, NY: Crowell, 1970.

  The Ellipse. New York, NY: Crowell, 1971.

Eberts, Marjorie & Margaret Gisler. *Pancakes, Crackers, and Pizza: A Book of Shapes.* Chicago, IL: Children's Press, 1984.

Ehlert, Lois. *Color Zoo.* New York, NY: Harper Collins Children's Books, 1989.

Emberley, Ed. *Ed Emberley's Picture Pie: A Circle Drawing Book.* Boston, MA: Little, Brown, 1984.

  The Wing on a Flea. New York, NY: Little, Brown, 1988.

Froman, Robert. *Angles Are Easy As Pie.* New York, NY: Crowell, 1975.

  Rubber Bands, Baseballs and Doughnuts. New York, NY: Crowell, 1972.

Gardner, Beau. *Guess What?: Text and Graphics.* New York, NY: Lothrop, Lee & Shepard Co., 1985.

Grifalconi, Ann. *The Village of Round and Square Houses.* New York, NY: Little, Brown, 1986.

Hoban, Tana. *Big Ones, Little Ones.* New York, NY: Greenwillow, 1976.

  Circles, Triangles and Squares. New York, NY: Macmillan Children's Group, 1974.

  Shapes, Shapes, Shapes. New York, NY: Greenwillow, 1986.

Jonas, Ann. *Round Trip.* New York, NY: Greenwillow, 1983.

Juster, Norton. *The Dot and the Line.* New York, NY: Random, 1963.

McDermott, Gerald. *Arrow to the Sun.* New York, NY: Puffin Books, 1977.

Nesbit, E. *Melisande.* San Diego, CA: Harcourt Brace, 1989.

Phillips, Jo. *Exploring Triangles: Paperfolding Geometry.* New York, NY: Crowell, 1975.

Reiss, John J. *Shapes.* New York, NY: Macmillan Children's Group, 1982.

Srivastava, Jane. *Spaces, Shapes and Sizes.* New York, NY: Crowell, 1980.

Sullivan, Janet. *Round Is a Pancake.* New York, NY: Holt, Rinehart & Winston, 1963.

Testa, Fulvio. *If You Look Around You.* New York, NY: Dial Books for Young Readers, 1987.

Tompert, Ann. *Grandfather Tang's Story.* New York, NY: Crown Publishers, 1990.

Graphing

Carlson, Nancy. *Harriet's Halloween Candy.* New York, NY: Puffin Books, 1984.

Caudill, Rebecca. *A Pocketful of Cricket.* New York, NY: H. Holt & Co., 1964.

Geringer, Laura. *A Three Day Hat.* New York, NY: Harper Collins Children's Books, 1987.

Papy, Frederique. *Graph Games.* New York, NY: Crowell, 1971.

Rice, Eve. *Peter's Pockets.* New York, NY: Greenwillow, 1989.

Slobodkin, Esphyr. *Caps For Sale.* New York, NY: Harper Collins Children's Books, 1987.

Large Numbers and Place Value

Anno, Mitsumasa. *Socrates and the Three Little Pigs.* New York, NY: Philomel Books, 1988.

Base, Graeme. *The Eleventh Hour.* Bergenfield, NJ: Abrams, 1993.

Birch, David. *The King's Chessboard.* New York, NY: Dial Books for Young Readers, 1988.

Cutler, Daniel Solomon. *One Hundred Monkeys.* New York, NY: S & S Trade, 1991.

Gag, Wanda. *Millions of Cats.* New York, NY: Scholastic, 1956.

Greene, Carol. *The Thirteen Days of Halloween.* Chicago, IL: Children's Press, 1983.

Karasz, Keiko. *The Wolf's Chicken Stew.* New York, NY: Putnam Publishing Group, 1989.

King, Olive. *Me and My Million.* New York, NY: Crowell, 1979.

MacCarthy, Patricia. *Ocean Parade.* New York, NY: Dial Books for Young Readers, 1990.

Martin, Jr., Bill. *The Happy Hippopotami.* San Diego, CA: Harcourt Brace, 1991.

McKissack, Patricia. *A Million Fish . . . More Or Less.* New York, NY: Knopf Books for Young Readers, 1992.

Rosenberg, Amye. *1 to 100 Busy Counting Book.* Racine, WI: Western Publishing Co., 1988.

Schwartz, David M. *How Much Is a Million?* New York, NY: Scholastic, 1985.

    If You Made a Million. New York, NY: Scholastic, 1989.

Trivas, Irene. *Emma's Christmas.* New York, NY: Orchard Books Watts, 1992.

Logic

Anno, Mitsumasa. *Anno's Hat Tricks.* New York, NY: Philomel Books, 1985.

    Topsy-Turvies: Pictures to Stretch the Imagination. New York, NY: Weatherhill, 1970.

    Upside-Downers. New York, NY: Weatherhill, 1971.

Froman, Robert. *Venn Diagrams.* New York, NY: Crowell, 1972.

Shannon, George. *More Stories to Solve: Folktales From Around the World.* New York, NY: Morrow, 1991.

    Stories to Solve: Fifteen Folktales From Around the World. New York, NY: Morrow, 1991.

Measurement

Adams, Pam. *Ten Beads Tall.* New York, NY: Child's Play, 1989.

Allen, Pam. *Who Sank the Boat?* New York, NY: Coward - McCann, Inc., 1982.

Anno, Mitsumasa. *The King's Flower.* New York, NY: Putnam Publishing Group, 1979.

Briggs, Raymond. *Jim and the Beanstalk.* New York, NY: Putnam Publishing Group, 1979.

Calmenson, Stephanie. *The Principal's New Clothes.* New York, NY: Scholastic, 1991.

Cantieni, Benita. *Little Elephant and Big Mouse.* Boston, MA: Picture Book Studio, 1981.

Caple, Kathy. *The Biggest Nose.* Boston, MA: Houghton Mifflin, 1985.

Carle, Eric. *Papa, Please Get the Moon for Me.* Boston, MA: Picture Book Studio, 1991.

    The Very Hungry Caterpillar. New York, NY: Scholastic, 1987.

Dahl, Roald. *Esio Trot.* New York, NY: Viking Children's Books, 1990.

Eastman, Philip D. *Big Dog, Little Dog: A Bedtime Story.* New York, NY: Random Books for Young Readers, 1973.

Farber, Norma. *As I Was Crossing Boston Common.* New York, NY: Puffin Books, 1991.

Fujikawa, Gyo. "The Crow and the Pitcher," "The Sun and the Wind," "The Wonderful Porridge Pot," "Why Evergreens Keep Their Leaves," in *Fairy Tales and Fables.* New York, NY: Putnam Publishing Group, 1970.

Galdone, Paul. *The Three Billy Goats Gruff.* Boston, MA: Houghton Mifflin, 1981.

Ginsburg, Mirra. *Mushroom in the Rain.* New York, NY: Macmillan Children's Group, 1990.

Grimes, Nikki. *Something On My Mind.* New York, NY: Dial Books for Young Readers, 1986.

Hall, Crowell. *Telltime the Rabbit.* New York, NY: Crowell, 1945.

Kaufman, Joe. *Big and Little.* Auburn, ME: Ladybird Books, 1992.

Kellogg, Steven. *Much Bigger Than Martin.* New York, NY: Dial Books for Young Readers, 1976.

Kitchen, Bert. *Animal Alphabet.* New York, NY: Puffin Books, 1988.

Leaf, Munro. *The Story of Ferdinand.* New York, NY: Puffin Books, 1993.

Lionni, Leo. *Inch By Inch.* New York, NY: Scholastic, 1960.

Lopshire, Robert. *The Biggest, Smallest, Fastest, Tallest Things You've Ever Heard Of.* New York, NY: Crowell, 1980.

Lord, John Vernon. *The Giant Jam Sandwich.* Boston, MA: Houghton Mifflin, 1987.

McMillan, Bruce. *Super, Super, Superwords.* New York, NY: Lothrop, 1989.

Morimoto, Junko. *The Inch Boy and Fables.* New York, NY: Puffin Books, 1988.

Myller, Rolf. *How Big Is a Foot?* New York, NY: Dell, 1991.

Nesbit, E. *Melisande.* San Diego, CA: Harcourt Brace, 1989.

Smith-Moore, J.J. *Sally Small.* Los Angeles, CA: Price, Stern & Sloan, 1988.

Tyron, Leslie. *Albert's Alphabet.* New York, NY: Macmillan Children's Group, 1991.

Miscellaneous

Reimer, Luetta & Wilbert Reimer. *Mathematicians Are People Too: Stories from the Lives of Great Mathematicians.* Palo Alto, CA: Seymour Publications, 1990.

Studio, D. *Crazy Creature Number Puzzles.* New York, NY: Sterling Publishing Co., 1986.

Money

Brenner, Barbara. *The Five Pennies.* New York, NY: Knopf, 1964.

Day, Alexandra. *Frank and Earnest.* New York, NY: Scholastic, 1988.

Hoban, Tana. *Twenty-six Letters and Ninety-nine Cents.* New York, NY: Scholastic, 1987.

Leedy, Loreen. *The Monster Money Book.* New York, NY: Holiday, 1992.

Lobel, Arnold & Anita. *On Market Street.* New York, NY: Morrow, 1989.

Maestro, Betsy. *The Story of Money.* New York, NY: Clarion Books, 1993.

Mathis, Sharon Bell. *The Hundred Penny Box.* New York, NY: Puffin, 1986.

Merrill, Jean. *The Toothpaste Millionaire.* Boston, MA: Houghton Mifflin, 1974.

Schwartz, David A. *If You Made a Million.* New York, NY: Scholastic, 1989.

Silverstein, Shel. "Smart" in *Where the Sidewalk Ends.* New York, NY: Harper Collins Children's Books, 1974.

Viorst, Judith. *Alexander, Who Used to Be Rich Last Sunday.* Hartford, CT: Atheneum, 1978.

Williams, Vera B. *A Chair For My Mother.* New York, NY: Morrow, 1993.

Zemach, Harve & Margot Aemach. *A Penny A Look.* New York, NY: FS & G, 1989.

Multiplication and Division

Aker, Suzanne. *What Comes In 2's, 3's, and 4's?* New York, NY: S & S Trade, 1990.

Anno, Masaichiro & Mitsumasa Anno. *Anno's Mysterious Multiplying Jar.* New York, NY: Philomel Books, 1983.

Dubanevich, Arlene. *Pigs in Hiding.* New York, NY: Scholastic, 1989.

Hutchins, Pat. *The Doorbell Rang.* New York, NY: Scholastic, 1986.

Mathews, Louise. *Bunches and Bunches of Bunnies.* New York, NY: Scholastic, 1991.

Pinczes, Elinor J. *One Hundred Hungry Ants.* Boston, MA: Houghton Mifflin, 1993.

Williams, Vera B. *A Chair For My Mother.* New York, NY: Morrow, 1994.

Number Concepts and Relationships

Adler, Irvin. *Mathematics.* New York, NY: Doubleday, 1990.

Anno, Mitsumasa. *Anno's Math Games.* New York, NY: Philomel Books, 1987.

Anno's Math Games II. New York, NY: Philomel Books, 1989.

Anno's Math Games III. New York, NY: Philomel Books, 1991.

Bang, Molly. *Ten, Nine, Eight.* New York, NY: Scholastic, 1993.

Becker, John. *Seven Little Rabbits.* New York, NY: Scholastic, 1991.

Carona, Philip. *Numbers.* Chicago, IL: Children's Press, 1982.

Dragonwagon, Cresent. *I Hate My Brother Harry.* San Francisco, CA: Harper & Row, 1983.

Galdone, Paul. *The Three Bears.* Boston, MA: Houghton Mifflin, 1985.

James, Elizabeth, & Carol Barkin. *What Do You Mean By "Average"?* New York, NY: Lothrop, Lee & Shepard, 1978.

Juster, Norton. *The Phantom Tollbooth.* New York, NY: Knopf Books for Young Readers, 1993.

Larrick, Nancy. *Cats Are Cats.* New York, NY: Putnam Publishing Group, 1988.

Lottridge, Celia Barker. *One Watermelon Seed.* New York, NY: OUP, 1990.

Luce, Marnie. *Infinity: What Is It?* Minneapolis, MN: Lerner Publications, 1969.

Sets: What Are They? Minneapolis, MN: Lerner Publications, 1969.

McGovern, Ann. *Stone Soup.* New York, NY: Macmillan Children's Group, 1986.

Ormerod, Jan. *101 Things To Do With a Baby.* New York, NY: Morrow, 1994.

Singletary, Helen P. *Understanding Numbers.* Charleston, SC: Computer Training Clinic, Inc., 1991.

Sitomer, Mindell. *How Did Numbers Begin?* New York, NY: Harper Collins Children's Books, 1976.

Sitomer, Mindell & Harry Sitomer. *Zero is Not Nothing.* New York, NY: Crowell, 1978.

Srivastava, Jane. *Number Families.* New York, NY: Crowell, 1979.

Thornhill, Jan. *The Wildlife 1 2 3, A Nature Counting Book.* New York, NY: S & S Trade, 1990.

Watson, Clyde. *Binary Numbers.* New York, NY: Harper Collins Children's Books, 1977.

Zaslavsky, Claudia. *Zero: Is It Something? Is It Nothing?* New York, NY: Watts, 1989.

Numeration and Counting

Aker, Suzanne. *What Comes In 2's, 3's, and 4's?* New York, NY: S & S Trade, 1992.

From *Writing Math: A Project-Based Approach*, published by GoodYear Books. Copyright © 1995 Sharon Z. Drazmin

Anno, Mitsumasa. *Anno's Counting Book.* New York, NY: Harper Collins Children's Books, 1986.

Aylesworth, James. *One Crow: A Counting Rhyme.* New York, NY: Harper Collins Children's Books, 1990.

Baum, Arline and Joseph. *One Bright Monday Morning.* New York, NY: Random House, 1973.

Berenstain, Stan & Janice. *Bears on Wheels.* New York, NY: Random Books for Young Readers, 1969.

Bishop, Claire Huchet. *The Five Chinese Brothers.* New York, NY: Putnam Publishing Group, 1989.

Twenty-Two Bears. New York, NY: Viking Press, 1964.

Blumenthal, Nancy. *Count-A-Saurus.* New York, NY: Macmillan Children's Group, 1989.

Brown, Marc, ed. *Hand Rhymes.* New York, NY: Dutton Children's Books, 1985.

Brustlein, Daniel. *One, Two, Three, Going to Sea: An Adding and Subtracting Book.* Reading, MA: Young Scott Books, 1964.

Bucknall, Caroline. *One Bear All Alone.* New York, NY: Dial Books for Young Readers, 1989.

Burmingham, John. *Hey! Get Off Our Train.* New York, NY: Crown Books for Young Readers, 1990.

Calemenson, Stephanie. *Ten Items or Less: A Counting Book.* Racine, WI: Golden Books, 1985.

Carle, Eric. *My Very First Book of Numbers.* New York, NY: Harper Collins Children's Books, 1985.

One, Two, Three to the Zoo. New York, NY: Putnam Publishing Group, 1990.

The Rooster Who Set Out to See the World. Boston, MA: Picture Book Studio, 1992.

Carter, David A. *How Many Bugs in a Box!* New York, NY: S & S Trade, 1988.

Cave, Kathryn & Chris Riddel. *Out for the Count: A Counting Adventure.* New York, NY: S & S Trade, 1992.

Clements, Andrew. *Mother Earth's Counting Book.* Boston, MA: Picture Book Studio, 1992.

Clifton, Lucille. *Everett Anderson's 1, 2, 3.* New York, NY: H. Holt & Co., 1992.

Crews, Donald. *Ten Black Dots.* New York, NY: Greenwillow, 1986.

Cristelow, Eileen. *Five Little Monkeys Jumping on the Bed.* Boston, MA: Houghton Mifflin, 1993.

Five Little Monkeys Sitting on a Tree. Boston, MA: Houghton Mifflin, 1993.

Crowther, Robert. *The Most Amazing Hide-and-Seek Counting Book.* New York, NY: Viking Children's Books, 1981.

Dee, Ruby. *Two Ways to Count to Ten.* New York, NY: Greenwillow, 1968.

Demi. *Demi's Count the Animals 1, 2, 3.* New York, NY: Putnam Publishing Group, 1990.

Du Bois, William P. *The Twenty-One Balloons.* New York, NY: Puffin Books, 1986.

Dunbar, Joyce. *Ten Little Mice.* San Diego, CA: Harcourt Brace, 1992.

Duvoisin, Roger. *Two Lonely Ducks: A Counting Book.* New York, NY: Knopf, 1955.

Ehlert, Lois. *Fish Eyes: A Book You Can Count On.* San Diego, CA: Harcourt Brace, 1992.

Eichenberg, Fritz. *Dancing in the Moon: Counting Rhymes*. San Diego, CA: Harcourt Brace, 1975.

Elkin, Benjamin. *Six Foolish Fishermen*. Chicago, IL: Children's Press, 1957.

Emberly, Barbara. *One Wide River to Cross*. New York, NY: Little, 1992.

Estes, Eleanor. *The Hundred Dresses*. San Diego, CA: Harcourt Brace, 1974.

Faulkner, Keith. *My Counting Book*. Basingstoke, Hants (England): Brainwaves Ltd., 1993.

Feelings, Muriel. *Moja Means One: A Swahili Counting Book*. New York, NY: Dial Books for Young Readers, 1987.

Game, S. T. & Lisa Erte. *One White Sail*. New York, NY: S & S Trade, 1993.

Giganti, Jr., Paul. *Each Orange Had 8 Slices*. New York, NY: Morrow, 1994.

    How Many Snails? New York, NY: Greenwillow, 1988.

Goennel, Heidi. *Odds and Evens: A Numbers Book*. New York, NY: Morrow, 1994.

Grossman, Virginia. *Ten Little Rabbits*. San Francisco, CA: Chronicle Books, 1991.

Hague, Kathleen. *Numbears: A Counting Book*. New York, NY: H. Holt & Co., 1986.

Hamm, Diane Johnston. *How Many Feet in the Bed?* New York, NY: S & S Trade, 1991.

Hammond, Franklin. *Ten Little Ducks*. New York, NY: Scholastic, 1993.

Haskins, James. *Count Your Way Through Africa*. Minneapolis, MN: Carolrhoda Books, 1989.

    Count Your Way Through Canada. Minneapolis, MN: Carolrhoda Books, 1989.

    Count Your Way Through China. Minneapolis, MN: Carolrhoda Books, 1987.

    Count Your Way Through Germany. Minneapolis, MN: Carolrhoda Books, 1991.

    Count Your Way Through India. Minneapolis, MN: Carolrhoda Books, 1992.

    Count Your Way Through Israel. Minneapolis, MN: Carolrhoda Books, 1990.

    Count Your Way Through Italy. Minneapolis, MN: Carolrhoda Books, 1990.

    Count Your Way Through Japan. Minneapolis, MN: Carolrhoda Books, 1987.

    Count Your Way Through Korea. Minneapolis, MN: Carolrhoda Books, 1989.

    Count Your Way Through Mexico. Minneapolis, MN: Carolrhoda Books, 1989.

    Count Your Way Through Russia. Minneapolis, MN: Carolrhoda Books, 1987.

    Count Your Way Through the Arab World. Minneapolis, MN: Carolrhoda Books, 1987.

Hawkins, Colin & Jacqui Hawkins. *When I Was One*. New York, NY: Viking, 1990.

Hayes, Sarah. *Nine Ducks Nine*. New York, NY: Lothrop, 1990.

Howard. Katherine. *I Can Count to One Hundred . . . Can You?* New York, NY: Random Books for Young Readers, 1979.

Hrada, Joyce. *It's the 0-1-2-3 Book*. Torrance, CA: Heian International, 1985.

Hulme, Joy. *Sea Squares*. New York, NY: Hyperion Books for Children, 1991.

Ifrah, Georges. *From One to Zero - A Universal History of Numbers*. New York, NY: Viking, 1985.

Ipcar, Dehlov Zorach. *Brown Cow Farm*. New York, NY: Doubleday, 1959.

    Ten Big Farms. New York, NY: Knopf, 1958.

Johnston, Tony. *Whale Song*. New York, NY: Putnam Publishing Group, 1987.

Kahl, Virginia. *How Many Dragons are Behind the Door?* New York, NY: Scribner, 1977.

Keats, Ezra Jack. *Over in the Meadow.* New York, NY: Scholastic, 1991.

Kherdian, David & Nonny Hogrogian. *The Cat's Midsummer Jamboree.* New York, NY: Philomel Books, 1990.

Kitamura, Satoshi. *When Sheep Cannot Sleep.* New York, NY: FS & G, 1986.

Kitchen, Bert. *Animal Numbers.* New York, NY: Dial Books for Young Readers, 1987.

Kredenser, Gail & Stanley Mack. *One Dancing Drum: A Counting Book for Children and Parents Who are Tired of Puppies & Chickens & Horses.* Chatham, NY: S.G. Phillips, 1971.

LeSieg, Theo. *Ten Apples Up On Top!* New York, NY: Beginner Books, 1961.

Lionni, Leo. *Frederick.* New York, NY: Knopf Books for Young Readers, 1973.

Livermore, Elaine. *One to Ten, Count Again.* La Puente, CA: J. Alden, 1972.

Mack, Stanley. *Ten Bears in My Bed: A Goodnight Countdown.* New York, NY: Pantheon, 1974.

Martin, Bill. *Monday, Monday, I Like Monday.* New York, NY: Holt, Rinehart & Winston, 1970.

Ten Little Squirrels. New York, NY: Holt, Rinehart & Winston, 1970.

Matthews, Louise. *Bunches and Bunches of Bunnies.* New York, NY: Scholastic, 1993.

Mayer, Marianna & Gerald McDermott. *The Brambleberrys Animal Book of Counting.* Honesdale, PA: Boyds Mill Press, 1991.

Mc Fadzean, Anita. *One Special Star.* New York, NY: S & S Trade, 1991.

McInnes, John. *Ducks Can't Count.* Watertown, MA: Charlesbridge Publishers, 1991.

McKee, Craig & Margaret Holland. *The Teacher Who Could Not Count.* St Petersburg, FL: Willowisp, 1986.

McLerran, Alice. *The Mountain That Loved a Bird.* Boston, MA: Picture Book Studio, 1991.

McMillan, Bruce. *One, Two, One Pair!* New York, NY: Scholastic, 1991.

Milne, A. A. *Pooh's Counting Book.* New York, NY: Dutton, 1982.

Moncure, Jane. *My Six Book.* Plymouth, MN: Child's World, 1986.

Moore, Inga. *Six-Dinner Sid.* New York, NY: S & S Trade, 1993.

Moss, Jeffrey. *People in My Family.* Racine, WI: Western Publishing Co., 1976.

Nelson, JoAnne. *Count By Twos.* New York, NY: McClanahan Books, 1990.

O'Donnell, Elizabeth Lee. *The Twelve Days of Summer.* New York, NY: Morrow Junior Books, 1991.

Pallotta, Jerry. *The Icky Bug Counting Book.* Watertown, MA: Charlesbridge Publishers, 1991.

Peek, Merle. *Roll Over! A Counting Song.* Boston, MA: Houghton Mifflin, 1981.

Peppe, Rodney. *Circus Numbers: A Counting Book.* New York, NY: Delacorte, 1985.

Pomerantz, Charlotte. *One Duck, Another Duck.* New York, NY: Greenwillow, 1984.

Quackenbush, Robert M. *Poems for Counting.* New York, NY: Holt, 1963.

Reiss, John J. *Numbers.* New York, NY: Macmillan Children's Group, 1987.

Samton, Sheila White. *Moon to Sun: An Adding Book.* Honesdale, PA: Boyds Mill Press, 1991.

On the River: An Adding Book. Honesdale, PA: Boyds Mill Press, 1991.

The World From My Window. Honesdale, PA: Boyds Mill Press, 1991.

Sanderson, Ruth. *The Twelve Dancing Princesses.* New York, NY: Little, 1993.

Scarry, Richard. *Richard Scarry's Best Counting Book Ever.* New York, NY: Random Books for Young Readers, 1975.

Scott, Ann Herbert. *One Good Horse: A Cowpuncher's Counting Book.* New York, NY: Greenwillow, 1990.

Seignobosc, Francoise. *Jean-Marie Counts Her Sheep.* New York, NY: Scribner, 1951.

Selfridge, Oliver. *Fingers Come in Fives.* Boston, MA: Houghton Mifflin, 1966.

Sendak, Maurice. *One Was Johnny.* New York, NY: Harper Collins Children's Books, 1991.

Seven Little Monsters. New York, NY: Harper Collins Children's Books, 1977.

Serfozo, Mary. *Who Wants One?* New York, NY: Macmillan Children's Group, 1992.

Sesame Street. *The Count's Counting Book.* New York, NY: Random Books for Young Readers, 1980.

Seuss, Dr. *One Fish, Two Fish, Red Fish, Blue Fish.* New York, NY: Random Books for Young Readers, 1960.

The 500 Hats of Bartholomew Cubbins. New York, NY: Random Books for Young Readers, 1989.

Sheppard, Jeff. *The Right Number of Elephants.* New York, NY: Scholastic, 1990.

Slater, Teddy. *Molly's Monsters.* New York, NY: Putnam Publishing Group, 1988.

Slobodkin, Esphyr. *Caps For Sale.* New York, NY: Harper Collins Children's Books, 1987.

Slobodkin, Louis. *One Is Good, But Two Are Better.* New York, NY: Vanguard Press, 1956.

Thaler, Mike. *Seven Little Hippos.* New York, NY: S & S Trade, 1991.

Thornhill, Jan. *The Wildlife 1-2-3: A Nature Counting Book.* New York, NY: S & S Trade, 1990.

Travis, Irene. *Emma's Christmas: An Old Song Resung and Pictured.* New York, NY: Orchard Books Watts, 1992.

Tudor, Tasha. *1 is One.* New York, NY: Macmillan Children's Group, 1988.

Wadsworth, Olivia and Mary M. McRae. *Over in the Meadow.* New York, NY: Viking Children's Books, 1985.

Wahl, John & Stacey Wahl. *I Can Count the Petals of a Flower.* Reston, VA: National Council of Teachers of Mathematics (NCTM), 1985.

Watson, Amy. *The Folk Art Counting Book.* New York, NY: Harry N. Abrams, Inc., Publishers, 1992.

Wildsmith, Brian. *One, Two, Three.* New York, NY: Oxford University Press, 1987.

Wood, Audrey & Don Wood. *Piggies.* San Diego, CA: Harcourt Brace, 1991.

Wood, Jakki. *One Tortoise, Ten Wallabies: A Wildlife Counting Book.* New York, NY: Bradbury Press, 1994.

Wylie, Joanne. *A More or Less Fish Story.* Chicago, IL: Children's Press, 1984.

How Many Monsters? Tulsa, OK: Educational Development Corp. (EDC), 1986.

Zaslavsky, Claudia. *Count on Your Fingers African-Style.* New York, NY: Harper Collins Children's Books, 1980.

Ziefert, Harriet. *A Dozen Dogs: A Read-and-Count Story.* New York, NY: Random Books for Young Readers, 1985.

Where's the Halloween Treat? New York, NY: Puffin Books, 1985.

Zolotow, Charlotte. *One Step, Two.* New York, NY: Lothrop, Lee & Shepard Books, 1981.

Patterns

Carle, Eric. *Animals, Animals.* New York, NY: Philomel Books, 1989.

Cleveland, David. *April Rabbits.* New York, NY: Scholastic, 1986.

Dahl, Roald. *Esio Trot.* New York, NY: Viking Children's Books, 1990.

Emberley, Ed. *Ed Emberley's A B C.* New York, NY: Little, Brown, 1978.

Hoban, Tana. *Look Up, Look Down.* New York, NY: Greenwillow, 1992.

Hutchins, Pat. *Don't Forget the Bacon!* New York, NY: Greenwillow, 1994.

Rosie's Walk. New York, NY: Macmillan Children's Group, 1971.

Kalan, Robert. *Jump, Frog, Jump.* New York, NY: Scholastic, 1991.

Mahy, Margaret. *17 Kings and 42 Elephants.* New York, NY: Dial Books for Young Readers, 1987.

Martin, Bill Jr. *Brown Bear, Brown Bear, What Do You See?* New York, NY: H. Holt & Co., 1983.

McClintock, Marshall. *A Fly Went By.* New York, NY: Beginner Books, 1958.

Provensen, Alice and Martin. *A Peaceable Kingdom, The ShakerABECEDARIUS.* New York, NY: Puffin Books, 1981.

Shaw, Charles Green. *It Looked Like Spilt Milk.* New York, NY: Harper Collins Children's Books, 1988.

Silverstein, Shel. *A Giraffe and a Half.* New York, NY: Harper Collins Children's Books, 1964.

Xiong, Blia. *Nine-In-One Grr! Grr!* Emeryville, CA: Children's Book Press, 1993.

Time

Anno, Mitsumasa. *All in a Day.* New York, NY: Philomel Books, 1986.

Anno's Counting Book. New York, NY: Harper Collins Children's Books, 1992.

Behn, Harry. *All Kinds of Time.* San Diego, CA: Harcourt Brace, 1950.

Carle, Eric. *The Grouchy Ladybug.* New York, NY: Harper Collins Children's Books, 1986.

Carlstrom, Nancy W. *Jesse Bear, What Will You Wear?* New York, NY: Scholastic, 1986.

Clifton, Lucille. *Everett Anderson's Nine Month Long Year.* New York, NY: H. Holt & Co., 1988

Coleridge, Sara. *January Brings the Snow.* New York, NY: Doubleday, 1989.

Combs, Ann. *How Old Is Old?* Los Angeles, CA: Price Stern, 1988.

Galdone, Paul. *The Little Red Hen.* Boston, MA: Clarion Books, 1985.

Gibbons, Gail. *Clocks and How They Go.* New York, NY: Crowell, 1979.

Sun Up, Sun Down. San Diego, CA: Harcourt Brace, 1987.

The Seasons of Arnold's Apple Tree. San Diego, CA: Harcourt Brace, 1984.

Gray, Nigel. *A Country Far Away.* New York, NY: Orchard Books Watts, 1991.

Hawkins, Collin. *What Time Is It, Mr. Wolf?* Auburn, ME: Ladybird Books, 1987.

Hutchins, Pat. *Clocks and More Clocks.* New York, NY: Macmillan Children's Group, 1994.

Lloyd, David. *The Stopwatch*. New York, NY: Lippincott, 1986.

Lundell, Margo. *Mouse's Book of Months*. New York, NY: Grosset & Dunlap, 1987.

Provensen, Alice & Martin. *The Year at Maple Hill Farm*. New York, NY: Macmillan Children's Group, 1988.

Sendak, Maurice. *Chicken Soup With Rice*. New York, NY: Harper Collins Children's Books, 1962.

Shulevitz, Uri. *One Monday Morning*. New York, NY: Macmillan Children's Group, 1974.

Simon, Carly. *Amy the Dancing Bear*. New York, NY: Doubleday, 1989.

Singer, Marilyn. *Nine O'Clock Lullaby*. New York, NY: Scholastic, 1991.

Slobodkin, Louis. *The Late Cuckoo*. New York, NY: Vanguard Press, 1962.

Ungerer, Tomi. *Moon Man*. New York, NY: Delacorte, 1991.

Viorst, Judith. *Alexander and the Terrible, Horrible, No Good, Very Bad Day*. New York, NY: Scholastic, 1972.

Ward, Cindy. *Cookie's Week*. New York, NY: Scholastic, 1988.

White, E. B. *Charlotte's Web*. New York, NY: Scholastic, 1952.

Williams, Vera B. *Three Days on a River in a Red Canoe*. New York, NY: Greenwillow, 1981.

Zolotow, Charlotte. *Over and Over*. New York, NY: Harper Collins Children's Books, 1952.